The CAULIFLOWER COOKBOOK

The CAULIFLOWER COOKBOOK

HEALTHY LOW-CARB SNACKS, SOUPS, SALADS, APPETIZERS, PASTAS, PIZZAS, PASTRIES, AND DINNERS

LEANNE KITCHEN

Skyhorse Publishing

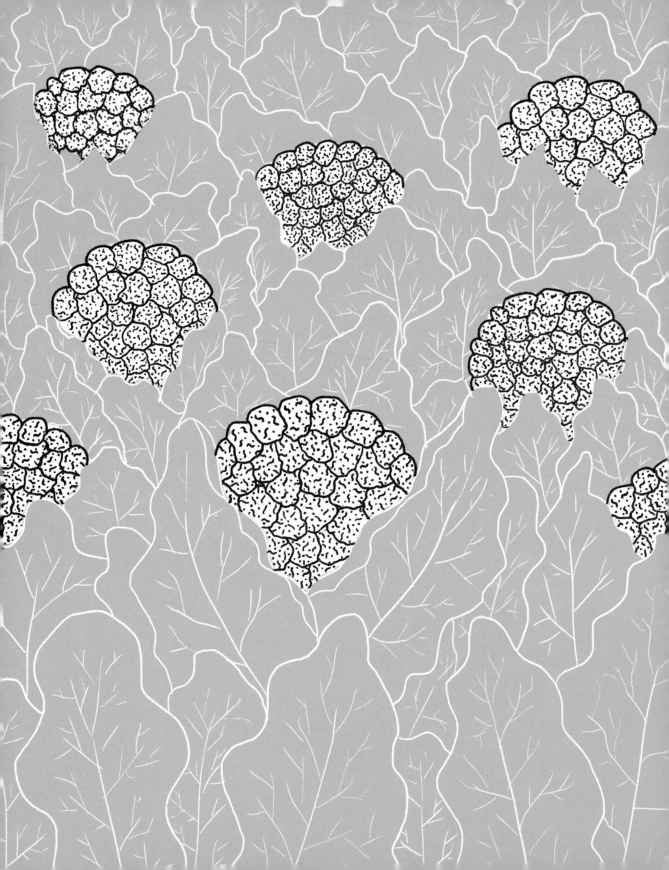

CONTENTS

INTRODUCTION TO CAULIFLOWER

Big and boofy, there's nothing quite like a cauliflower. And it seems the world is realizing exactly that—it's fair to say that this king of vegetables is having something of a "zeitgeist moment" right now. As a variety of *Brassica oleracea*, cauliflower is closely related to broccoli (another vegetable unusual for the fact that we eat the flower) and is reckoned to have evolved from wild cabbage. Its characteristic appearance is actually the result of arrested development—the normal forming of flower and stalk is interrupted, causing the immature flower heads to accumulate in a large mass. In this, the cauli is somewhat unique, although it does have plenty of other brassica family members: broccoli, cabbage, kale, kohlrabi, Brussels sprouts and Chinese broccoli—even turnips, wasabi, arugula and horseradish—are all related to it. But in terms of looks, flavor and downright versatility, the cauliflower is pretty much out there on its own. With so many ways to prepare it, cauliflower has long been a kitchen stalwart.

FROM WHENCE THE CAULIFLOWER?

Before we get into the practicalities of cauli cooking and all the great things you can do with your favorite brassica, first a little background info. The name "cauliflower" literally means "cabbage flower" from the Latin *caulis* or "cabbage" and "flower" for, well, "flower." It's thought that cauliflowers initially popped up in Cyprus (although some reckon Egypt). Roman-era writer Pliny the Elder enthused about cauli in his first-century opus *Natural History*, wherein he pronounced it "the most pleasant-tasted (sic)" of "all the cabbages" (although it's likely he was describing an earlier form of the cauliflower, not the one we know and love today).

The Cyprus connection makes sense when one considers that the island went on to become an English colony; there's a theory that cauliflower made it to England in the seventeenth century from here, although some say it was introduced to Britain by Flemish weavers. Three varieties of cauliflower were written about in Spain in the twelfth century, although our modern version was first used in Italy when, around 1500, it blew into Genoa from either Cyprus or the Levant. From there it traveled to France sometime later in the sixteenth century, where it became wildly popular in the court of Louis XIV. It was considered a delicacy, and the French aristocracy slathered it in ridiculously rich sauces, packed with palace favorites such as cream, foie gras, sweetbreads, ham and mushrooms.

An interesting relic from French culinary history is that the words "du Barry" denote cauliflower dishes in the classical cooking repertoire. This is after Madame du Barry, a French courtesan during the reign of Louis XV. It's not agreed how she came to be so closely connected with cauliflower, but crème du Barry, for example, is still a posh way of saying "cauliflower soup." Hypotheses for the association include that her white powdered hair-do resembled cauliflower curds, and that her pale complexion was cauliflower-like in color. Madame du Barry met her fate at the blade of the guillotine during the French Revolution. "Let them eat brassica"?

From Europe to the rest of the world? Interestingly, cauliflower didn't become commercially available in America until the 1920s. One cuisine that does have a prodigious number of cauliflower recipes is India (the Brits introduced it there) and now India is second only to China as the largest grower of the vegetable king.

KING OF CURDS

The edible part of cauliflower is composed of tightly clustered florets that are usually, but not always, white—more on that later. These are called the "curd." Enclosed by tight green leaves, the curd is considered the business end of the cauli, though you can happily eat the stalk and the long, pale green leaves that hug it. Mostly though, the leaves are hacked off before you buy, which is a shame. As well as tasting great, they're a good indicator of freshness—they should be pert and tight, not floppy. When the cauliflower is in the ground, the leaves draw up to cover the curd, protecting it from sunlight and preventing it from producing chlorophyll and turning green. Hence . . . whiteness.

Cauliflowers are notoriously tricky to grow, which might explain why they're never bargain-basement cheap. An autumn/winter crop (although you can buy them year round thanks to modern agriculture), they're sensitive to extreme cold, as well as extreme heat, and don't like sudden changes in temperature or rainfall. They're also picky about their soil, although new hybrids are less sensitive.

So, let's assume that, unless you're an ace gardener, you're buying your cauliflowers. When you do, choose those that feel heavy and compact and have an unblemished, creamy and tight curd. The curd should not be blindingly bright white, as this signifies the vegetable is not yet fully mature. Any loose or discolored curds tell you the cauli is past its best. Buy whole cauliflowers rather than pre-cut, if you can avoid them. An uncut cauli will keep longer—up to seven days in an open plastic bag in the crisper section of the fridge—whereas cut florets will only be good for a few days. Store a whole cauliflower stem down, as storing it head down can result in moisture accumulation, which causes it to spoil. Washing a cauliflower before you store it can also cause spoilage, so don't do that, either.

VARIATIONS ON A THEME

As for varieties, there are a few. A restaurant-driven trend for "baby" vegetables has given rise to cute tiny caulis recently; around the size of large tennis balls. These aren't mainstream though, so you'll be lucky to see them outside specialty produce stores.

Then there are purple cauliflowers, which get their color (the curds vary from light to dark mauve) from the presence of anthocyanin, the same pigment that is in red wine and red cabbage. A powerful antioxidant, anthocyanin is thought to deliver potent health

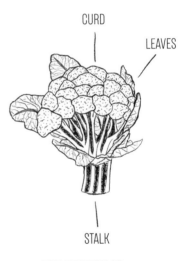

CURD

LEAVES

STALK

**THE ANATOMY OF
A CAULIFLOWER**

benefits. Purple cauliflower contains more vitamin A than white cauli.

The green cauliflower is also called Broccoflower, a trademarked name for a cross between broccoli and cauliflower. It looks just like a regular cauliflower, but with curds of pretty lime green. The romanesco cauliflower is also green but, instead of smooth curds, the florets are shaped into beautiful pointy lumps that range out in a swirly pattern from the central core. It's renowned in the scientific community for this "fractal" patterning, wherein the lovely pointy bits look exactly the same at every scale (some are big, some are small) and there are mathematical laws behind its incredible symmetry. Romanesco cauliflowers, first cultivated near Rome in the sixteenth century, are related to both cauliflower and broccoli. Creamy and nutty flavored, they don't have any of that slightly bitter edge those other two vegetables can sometimes have and, culinarily speaking, whatever you can do with a cauliflower, you can do with the romanesco version.

Last, but by no means least, there's an orange cauliflower, sometimes called the "cheddar cauliflower" on account of its vibrant orange curds. It first grew in Canada in 1970 and took decades of cross-breeding to develop as a fully fledged commercial variety. Its color comes from an extra burst of beta carotene (the same substance that makes carrots orange) and, while pretty, it doesn't taste any different to a regular cauliflower. But, scientists reckon it delivers a whopping 25 percent more vitamin A than regular, white cauli.

LOWEST CARBS IN TOWN

While we're speaking of health benefits, as well as being the lowest-carb vegetables there are, cauliflowers are also premium brain food due to the fact that they are rich in a nutrient called choline. Choline is essential for brain development—it helps to repair and maintain cell membranes.

It's also good to know that cauliflowers are an excellent source of dietary fiber, vitamins C, K and B group and minerals such as manganese, potassium, and magnesium. In fact, cauliflowers contain some of almost every vitamin and mineral your body needs. Cauliflowers also include glucosinolates, which are sulphur-containing compounds that break down into phytochemicals when you chew. These compounds inhibit enzymes that can activate carcinogens, help eliminate carcinogens from your body and are thought to suppress tumor development.

HOW TO KILL YOUR CAULIFLOWER IN THREE EASY LESSONS

Don't, for heaven's sake, overcook cauliflower—this will destroy all the vegetable's many nutrients. Studies have shown that prolonged cooking in water, in particular, decreases health benefits significantly. Throw in the fact that boiling is maybe the least appetizing way to prepare cauli and you've got an, er, watertight case against ever doing it. Boiling water gets trapped in cauliflower, making it mushy and a bit tasteless. Plus, that unpleasant, sulphury smell and taste you can get from cauliflower? It's from overcooking, particularly over-boiling. In the main, boiling should be avoided, unless you are trying keenly to re-create a 1970s school lunch. Roasting, steaming, sautéing, grilling and deep-frying (either coated or battered) are all good ways to cook your cauliflower; it can also be eaten raw.

THE RISE AND RISE OF THE KING

Unless you've been living in culinary seclusion, you'll have seen how, in recent years, very finely processed cauliflower is now being used as the main ingredient for pizza bases, cooked and served as a rice or couscous substitute, and even included in baked items like muffins. In fact, chefs tinkering with new ways to prepare cauliflower—as steaks; in ultra thin, raw slices; and dipped, battered and deep-fried, for example— have helped revolutionize cauliflower cookery in recent years.

But maybe they're just catching on to what cooks around the world have been doing for an age. While the Anglo-Saxon tradition gave rise to generations of boiling cauli and drowning it in cheese sauce (the latter not necessarily a bad thing, if done properly), Middle Eastern, Indian and Mediterranean cooks have taken more of a gastronomic high road with the vegetable. In Sicily, for example, they know that pan-roasting cauliflower in olive oil with anchovies, chopped raisins and garlic until it turns golden, sweet and completely collapses (see page 78), is a great way to make a sauce for pasta. In the Levant, deep-fried cauli, served with a tahini sauce for dipping, is standard delicious fare. Maqluba (see page 94) is a masterpiece of Palestinian cooking—a genius layered, one-pot dish of meat, rice, cauliflower, eggplant, spice and nuts. Then there's India, responsible, arguably, more than any other country for a mind blowing line-up of cauliflower dishes. From curries and flat bread stuffings to soups, pickles and fritters, these are the sort of cauliflower dishes you wish your mother knew about when she was busy filling the kitchen with the sulphuric smell of over-boiled brassica.

CAULI COOKING

Prepping and cooking cauliflower is really rather simple. Remove the outer leaves and the tough base, using the stems and leaves in any soup, steamed or stew recipes, if you like. (You can also roast or grill these whole leaves or sliced bases). Using a sharp knife, cut the cauliflower through the stem into naturally forming florets. The size depends on the recipe: they can be large, medium or small. Wash them and cut off any blemishes or soft bits. Medium-sized florets will take 5–7 minutes to steam and maybe 35 minutes to roast in the oven—they lose water and shrink when they're roasted, but in the process they turn golden, sweet and nutty-tasting and their flavor is a complete revelation if you've never cooked them this way before.

Grilling or barbecuing cauliflower accentuates its earthy flavors—the key to success at this is having your heat just right (not too hot or the cauli will incinerate) and the pieces not too thick, or they will never cook through. Some recipes will have you cut your cauli widthways into thick slices, or "steaks"—do this by slicing through the core. These can be barbecued, grilled or roasted in the oven and the core is essential to hold large pieces together.

When using cauliflower raw, very thinly sliced is the best way to go. Or process the florets in a food processor until very finely chopped (depending on the recipe). This is the way to make cauliflower "rice" too (see page 118)—you definitely require a food processor for this.

Otherwise, cooking with caulis can be decidedly lo-fi. A steamer, a grill pan or barbecue, a frying pan, saucepan or the oven are the usual routes to cauli tenderness. If you want to roast a cauliflower whole, it's best to parboil it first for about 15 minutes, depending on size, or it will take several hours to cook through in the oven.

WE WHO ARE ABOUT TO COOK, SALUTE YOU.

CONVERSION CHARTS

Metric and Imperial Conversions
(These conversions are rounded for convenience)

Ingredient	Cups/Tablespoons/Teaspoons	Ounces	Grams/Milliliters
Butter	1 cup/ 16 tablespoons/ 2 sticks	8 ounces	230 grams
Cheese, shredded	1 cup	4 ounces	110 grams
Cream cheese	1 tablespoon	0.5 ounce	14.5 grams
Cornstarch	1 tablespoon	0.3 ounce	8 grams
Flour, all-purpose	1 cup/1 tablespoon	4.5 ounces/0.3 ounce	125 grams/8 grams
Flour, whole wheat	1 cup	4 ounces	120 grams
Fruit, dried	1 cup	4 ounces	120 grams
Fruits or veggies, chopped	1 cup	5 to 7 ounces	145 to 200 grams
Fruits or veggies, pureed	1 cup	8.5 ounces	245 grams
Honey, maple syrup, or corn syrup	1 tablespoon	0.75 ounce	20 grams
Liquids: cream, milk, water, or juice	1 cup	8 fluid ounces	240 milliliters
Oats	1 cup	5.5 ounces	150 grams
Salt	1 teaspoon	0.2 ounce	6 grams
Spices: cinnamon, cloves, ginger, or nutmeg (ground)	1 teaspoon	0.2 ounce	5 milliliters
Sugar, brown, firmly packed	1 cup	7 ounces	200 grams
Sugar, white	1 cup/1 tablespoon	7 ounces/0.5 ounce	200 grams/12.5 grams
Vanilla extract	1 teaspoon	0.2 ounce	4 grams

Oven Temperatures

Fahrenheit	Celsius	Gas Mark
225°	110°	¼
250°	120°	½
275°	140°	1
300°	150°	2
325°	160°	3
350°	180°	4
375°	190°	5
400°	200°	6
425°	220°	7
450°	230°	8

MEASURES GUIDE

We have used Australian 20 ml (4 teaspoon) tablespoon measures. If you are using a smaller European 15 ml (3 teaspoon) tablespoon, add an extra teaspoon of the ingredient for each tablespoon specified.

SNAC
START
AND SO

KS,
ER'S,
JPS

Turn on the oven, throw in some spice and parmesan-slathered bits of cauliflower, bake until it's all gorgeously golden, then go find a movie to watch and dig in. Vary the seasonings to suit your taste—caraway seeds, for example, would work in place of the cumin and cilantro.

CAULIFLOWER POPCORN

Serves 4–6

40 g (1½ oz/¼ cup) sesame seeds
1½ teaspoons cumin seeds
2 teaspoons ground coriander
1½ teaspoons onion powder
100 g (3½ oz/1 cup) grated parmesan cheese
2 teaspoons sea salt
1 teaspoon freshly ground black pepper
1 kg (2 lb 4 oz/about 1 medium) cauliflower,
    trimmed and cut into 2 cm (¾ inch) pieces
4 tablespoons extra virgin olive oil

Preheat the oven to 180°C (350°F) and line three baking trays with parchment paper.

Combine the sesame seeds, cumin seeds, coriander, onion powder, parmesan, salt and pepper in a food processor and process to a coarse powder.

Spread the cauliflower on the baking trays and drizzle with olive oil. Toss to coat, then sprinkle with the parmesan mixture. Bake, stirring occasionally, for 25 minutes, then swap the trays and bake for another 25 minutes or until deep golden. Serve hot.

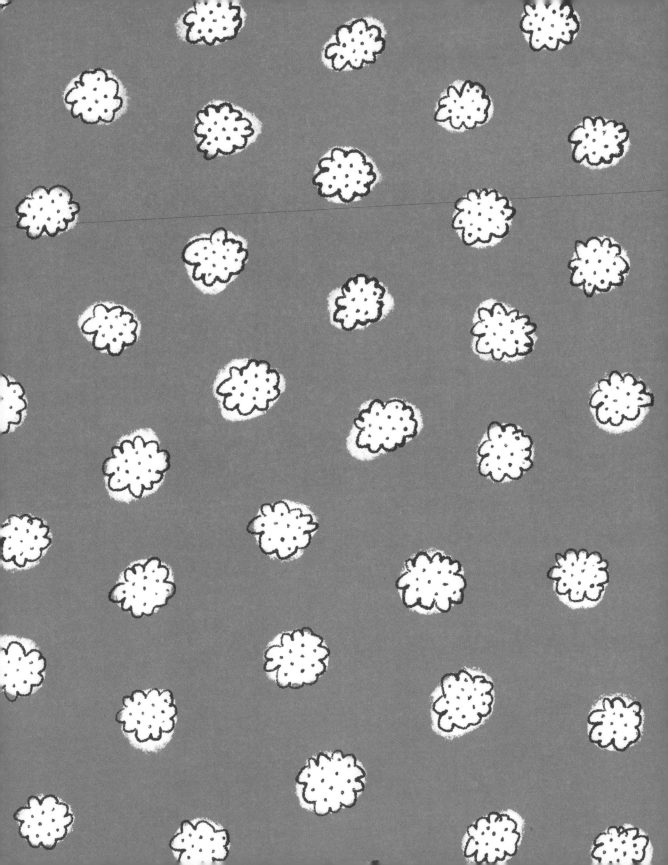

You can never have enough hummus recipes under your belt and so . . . cauliflower hummus. Buy some ready-to-go pita bread, olives and Lebanese pickles, throw them on a platter with a few slices of pastirma and bits of Turkish string cheese or feta, wedges of tomato, olives and slices of cucumber and, *voila* your mezze plate is sorted.

CAULIFLOWER HUMMUS

Serves 4–6

800 g (1 lb 12 oz/about 1 small) cauliflower, trimmed and cut into small florets
4 tablespoons extra virgin olive oil
2 garlic cloves, chopped
1 x 400 g (14-oz) can chickpeas, drained
1 teaspoon ground cumin
4 tablespoons tahini
2 tablespoons lemon juice, or to taste
2 tablespoons pine nuts, toasted
Sumac, to sprinkle
Pita bread, olives and Lebanese pickles etc, to serve

Preheat the oven to 180°C (350°F).

Place the cauliflower in a single layer on a large baking tray and drizzle with 2½ tablespoons of the oil. Roast for 30 minutes, stirring occasionally, or until the cauliflower is golden and tender. Cool slightly.

Reserve half the cauliflower and place the other half in a food processor with as much olive oil as you can pour off the tray. Add the garlic and process until smooth, then add the chickpeas, cumin, tahini, lemon juice, remaining olive oil and 3 tablespoons water. Process until the mixture is very smooth. Season to taste with sea salt and freshly ground black pepper, adding a little extra lemon juice if necessary.

Arrange in a serving bowl, then scatter with the reserved roast cauliflower and pine nuts. Sprinkle with sumac to taste, then serve with pita bread, olives and pickles.

This is what happens when you take the bread out of a cheese sandwich and replace it with . . . you guessed it . . . cauliflower. Serve with a salad on the side and you've got lunch or a light dinner, done and dusted. Divide this between two, instead of four, for a proper big meal.

CAULIFLOWER CHEESE "SANDWICHES"

Serves 4

1 kg (2 lb 4 oz/about 1 medium) cauliflower, trimmed
1 egg, beaten well
1 egg yolk
50 g (1¾ oz/½ cup) grated parmesan cheese
150 g (5½ oz/1½ cups) grated cheddar or mozzarella cheese

Cut the cauliflower into small pieces then, working in batches, process in a food processor until it is very finely chopped and resembles rice. Put in a large saucepan with 125 ml (4 fl oz/½ cup) water, cover tightly with a lid, then cook over medium–high heat, stirring often, for 5–6 minutes or until the cauliflower is tender. Transfer to a colander lined with a clean dish towel and cool slightly.

Preheat the oven to 180°C (350°F) and line a baking tray with parchment paper.

When the cauliflower is cool enough to handle, wrap it tightly in the towel so it can't spill out then, using your hands, squeeze very tightly to remove as much liquid as possible. It should feel dryish and be reduced in bulk. Mix well in a bowl with the egg, egg yolk, parmesan, salt and pepper.

Divide the mixture into four, even-sized portions, then spread each one on the baking tray, pressing it with your hands to form a neat 11 cm (4¼ inch) square. Use a large knife to push the edges square. Bake for 20–25 minutes or until set and light golden, turning the tray occasionally so the squares cook evenly. Remove from the oven and scatter the cheddar cheese evenly over two of the squares. Taking care not to break them, loosen the remaining two squares and place them on top of the cheese, to make sandwiches. Return to the oven and bake for another 8–10 minutes or until the cheese has melted. Cut in half and serve hot.

Ooooh, these are too good; even veggie-avoiding children like them. And they're simple to make. Just be sure to cut the vegetables very, very finely or they won't cook properly (or look good). Use your hands to work the vegetables through that batter-y mixture as it's uber thick and a wooden spoon simply won't cut it. Then, just drop loosely formed fritters into hot oil. Use carrot, potato or pumpkin instead of sweet potato if you prefer, and try adding a bit of extra onion too.

CAULIFLOWER BHAJIS

Makes about 16 bhajis

200 g (7 oz/about ½ medium) orange sweet potato
200 g (7 oz) cauliflower florets
1 onion
Vegetable oil, for deep-frying

BHAJI BATTER
200 g (7 oz/1⅔ cups) besan (chickpea flour)
60 ml (2 fl oz/¼ cup) Greek-style yogurt
1 tablespoon vegetable oil
1 teaspoon chili powder
1 teaspoon garam masala
1 teaspoon ground cumin
1½ teaspoons salt

CUCUMBER-MINT RAITA
2 Lebanese (short) cucumbers, trimmed and grated
1 teaspoon salt
375 ml (13 fl oz/1½ cups) Greek-style yogurt
Handful of mint leaves, chopped

For the cucumber-mint raita, place the cucumber in a strainer and sprinkle with salt. Leave for 20 minutes to drain, then squeeze out the excess liquid. Mix the cucumber in a bowl with the remaining ingredients. Add 1–2 table-spoons water to give a thick coating consistency. Season with black pepper and refrigerate.

Preheat the oven to 120°C (235°F).

For the bhaji batter, combine all the ingredients in a large bowl with 100 ml (3½ fl oz) cold water and stir until a smooth, very thick paste forms. Set aside.

Using a large, sharp knife, cut the sweet potato into very thin matchsticks. Very finely slice the cauliflower, including the stalks. Cut the onion in half lengthways, then very thinly slice. Add the vegetables to the batter then, using clean hands, work the vegetables through the batter.

Heat enough vegetable oil for deep-frying in a wok or large saucepan to 160°C (315°F) or until a cube of bread turns golden in 60 seconds. Working in batches, drop heaped tablespoons of the vegetable mixture into the oil and cook for 6–7 minutes, turning them once, or until deep golden, crisp and cooked through. Transfer to a large plate lined with paper towels and keep warm in the oven while you cook the rest. Serve with the raita for dipping.

Turks love red lentils, using them in soups and in these spicy little bites, although they don't put cauliflower in theirs. You can make the mixture in advance if you like, but don't roll it into balls until you're almost ready to serve or the kofte will dry out a bit.

CAULIFLOWER AND BURGHUL KOFTE

Serves 6

250 g (9 oz) cauliflower florets
140 g (5 oz/scant 1 cup) red lentils
2 tablespoons extra virgin olive oil, plus extra for serving
1 onion, finely chopped
2 garlic cloves, chopped
2 teaspoons sweet paprika
1½ teaspoons ground cumin
1½ teaspoons ground coriander
½ teaspoon dried chili flakes, or to taste
1½ tablespoons tomato paste (concentrated purée)
1½ tablespoons Turkish red pepper paste
150 g (5½ oz/scant 1 cup) fine burghul (bulgur)
1½ tablespoons lemon juice
Baby romaine lettuce leaves, to serve
Lemon wedges, to serve

Place the cauliflower in a food processor and process until very finely chopped. Combine the lentils in a saucepan with 330 ml (11¼ fl oz/1⅓ cups) water, bring to a simmer, then cover tightly and cook for 5 minutes. Add the cauliflower, cover and cook for about another 10 minutes or until the lentils and cauliflower are very tender and the liquid has been absorbed. Cool slightly.

Meanwhile, heat the oil in a saucepan over medium heat, add the onion and garlic and cook, stirring, for 5 minutes until the onion has softened. Add the spices and cook, stirring, for 1–2 minutes or until fragrant, then stir in the tomato and pepper pastes. Cook for another minute, then remove from the heat and stir into the lentil mixture.

Rinse the burghul in a bowl of cold water, drain well then, using your hands, squeeze to remove excess water. Add to the lentil mixture with the lemon juice and, using your hands, mix well, kneading the mixture until everything is combined and smooth. Season with sea salt and freshly ground black pepper.

Take about 1 slightly heaped tablespoon of the mixture and roll it into a ball. Using your finger, make an indentation in the middle of the ball. Repeat with the remaining mixture, then place the kofte in a single layer on a large platter and drizzle with olive oil. Serve with lettuce leaves for wrapping, and with lemon wedges for squeezing over the top.

If you don't want to make the grissini, toast your favorite bread in the oven (brush it with olive oil first) until it's crisp and use that instead. Or just buy some grissini. But like most things, making your own is better and, while many cooks run a mile from yeast, it's actually easy to use. So long as you don't put it in really hot water to begin with (it should be body-temperature tepid), you can't go too far wrong.

CAULIFLOWER AND PARMESAN DIP WITH GRISSINI

Serves 4–6

4 tablespoons extra virgin olive oil
600 g (1 lb 5 oz/about ½ medium) cauliflower, trimmed and cut into 2 cm (¾ inch) pieces
3 garlic cloves, finely chopped
1 bay leaf
125 ml (4 fl oz/½ cup) chicken or vegetable stock
1 x 400 g (14-oz) can white beans, drained and rinsed
80 g (2¾ oz/¾ cup) finely grated parmesan cheese

FENNEL AND PEPPER GRISSINI

150 ml (5 fl oz) lukewarm water
Large pinch of sugar
1 teaspoon instant dried yeast
1½ tablespoons extra virgin olive oil
1 teaspoon salt
225 g (8 oz/1½ cups) plain (all-purpose) flour
1 teaspoon fennel seeds, crushed lightly
3 teaspoons freshly ground black pepper

For the grissini, combine the water and sugar in a large bowl, sprinkle with the yeast, then leave for 5 minutes or until the yeast is foamy. Add the olive oil, salt, flour, fennel seeds and pepper and stir to form a coarse dough. Turn out onto a lightly floured board, then knead for 5–6 minutes or until smooth and elastic. Place in a lightly oiled bowl, cover with plastic wrap and leave in a draught-free place for 1¼ hours or until doubled in size.

Preheat the oven to 180°C (350°F).

Lightly grease a baking tray with oil. Use your hand to deflate the dough, then turn it out onto a lightly floured surface. Using a rolling pin, roll the dough out into a 22 x 34 cm (9 x 13 inch) rectangle. Turn the dough so a long edge is facing you, then use a large, sharp knife to cut into 26 strips. Use your hand to roll each strip into a thin log about 26 cm (10½ inches) long; some will be longer than others. Place on the tray and bake for 35 minutes or until golden and crisp. Transfer to a rack to cool.

Heat the oil over medium heat in a large saucepan. Stir in the cauliflower, garlic and bay leaf, cover and cook, stirring often, for 15 minutes or until starting to soften. Add the stock, cover and cook for another 10 minutes or until the cauliflower is very tender. Remove the bay leaf. Add the white beans, then remove from the heat and, using an immersion blender or food processor, process until smooth. Return to the heat, add the parmesan and stir over low heat until the mixture is heated through and the parmesan has melted. Season well and serve warm with the grissini.

Basically, you're making choux pastry here—the same pastry that's used to make chocolate eclairs and sweet profiteroles. But it can also be used to make fritters, both sweet and savory, and it works deliciously well with this combination of cauliflower, anchovies and parmesan. Yum.

CAULIFLOWER AND ANCHOVY BEIGNETS

Serves 4

800 g (1 lb 12 oz/about 1 small) cauliflower, trimmed
3 tablespoons olive oil
1 teaspoon salt
65 g (2¼ oz/¼ cup) softened unsalted butter, chopped
100 g (3½ oz/⅔ cup) plain (all-purpose) flour
4 eggs, beaten well
8 anchovy fillets, finely chopped
1½ teaspoons freshly ground black pepper
75 g (2½ oz/¾ cup) grated parmesan cheese
Vegetable oil, for deep-frying

Preheat the oven to 180°C (350°F).

Trim the base of the cauliflower, then cut the cauliflower through the stalks into pieces about 4 cm (1½ inches) across and about 1 cm (½ inch) thick. Place in a single layer on a large baking tray, drizzle with the olive oil and bake, turning occasionally, for 35 minutes or until golden and tender. Remove from the oven and cool. Reduce the oven temperature to 120°C (235°F).

For the batter, combine 170 ml (5½ fl oz/⅔ cup) water, the salt and butter in a saucepan and bring to the boil over medium heat. As soon as the mixture comes to the boil, add all the flour at once. Stir vigorously until the mixture is thick and smooth then continue cooking, stirring constantly, until the dough forms a ball that pulls away from the side of the pan. Remove from the heat and cool for 5 minutes. Transfer the mixture to a bowl, then, using electric beaters, beat in the egg a little at a time, beating well between each addition; the mixture should be smooth before adding more egg. Beat in the anchovy, pepper and parmesan.

Heat enough oil for deep-frying in a large saucepan to 160°C (315°F) or until a cube of bread turns golden in 60 seconds. Working in batches, dip the cauliflower in the batter, turning it to coat and gently scraping off excess batter. Don't worry if small parts of the cauliflower pieces are not completely covered. Fry for about 6 minutes, turning once, or until deep golden. Using a slotted spoon, transfer to a baking tray lined with paper towels to absorb excess oil. Place in the oven to keep warm while you cook the remaining fritters.

Caramelized . . . how? If you cook cauliflower for long enough in a little oil, its natural sugars will concentrate and become more pronounced, a.k.a. caramelize. Cauli cooked this way develops a sweet nuttiness that's quite intense and is the perfect foil for salty smoked salmon. It also works with prosciutto, which you could try here instead. Just skip the crème fraîche in that case, and garnish with basil leaves.

CARAMELIZED CAULIFLOWER AND SMOKED SALMON CROSTINI

Makes about 40 crostini

1 day-old baguette
Olive oil, for brushing
250 g (9 oz) smoked salmon
Crème fraîche and dill sprigs, to garnish

CARAMELIZED CAULIFLOWER

800 g (1 lb 12 oz/about 1 small) cauliflower, trimmed and cut into 1 cm (½ inch) pieces
60 ml (2 fl oz/¼ cup) extra virgin olive oil
2 tablespoons whole-egg mayonnaise

Preheat the oven to 180°C (350°F). Place the cauliflower in a baking dish in a single layer, drizzle with the olive oil and toss to coat well.

Bake for 40 minutes or until deep golden and very tender. Cool to room temperature, then transfer to a food processor with the mayonnaise. Process until the mixture is smooth, then season to taste with salt and pepper.

Cut the baguette into 1 cm (½ inch) thick slices and place on a baking tray in a single layer. Brush lightly with olive oil, then bake for about 15 minutes or until golden and crisp. Cool.

Spread the crostini thickly with the cauliflower mixture. Tear the salmon into small pieces and divide among the crostini. Spoon a little crème fraîche on to each, then top with a piece of dill. Serve immediately.

A chicken mayo sandwich with properly trimmed crusts (yes, an electric knife really is the best thing to use here) is the Little Black Dress of the entertaining world. Everyone loves to eat them and every cook should have a decent one in their repertoire. Cauliflower only makes them better. Homemade mayonnaise is fantastic, but if you want to use store-bought, make it a top-quality whole-egg variety.

CAULIFLOWER, CHICKEN AND CAPER SANDWICHES

Makes 24 small sandwiches

750 ml (26 fl oz/3 cups) chicken stock
1 large chicken breast (about 350 g/12 oz)
250 g (9 oz) small cauliflower florets
12 slices of fresh thin white bread
Softened butter, for spreading

CAPER AND TARRAGON MAYONNAISE
2 egg yolks
1 tablespoon Dijon mustard
1 tablespoon white wine vinegar
250 ml (9 fl oz/1 cup) olive oil
2 tablespoons drained baby capers
1½ tablespoons chopped tarragon

For the mayonnaise, combine the egg yolks, mustard and vinegar in a food processor and process until combined well. With the motor running, add the oil in a thin, steady stream until a thick, emulsified sauce forms—don't add it too fast or the mayonnaise may curdle. Stir in the capers and tarragon, season to taste with sea salt and freshly ground black pepper, then transfer to a bowl. Cover the surface with plastic wrap to prevent a skin forming.

Heat the chicken stock in a small saucepan over medium heat. When it begins to gently simmer, add the chicken breast then cook, covered, over medium–low heat for about 20 minutes or until it is nearly cooked through. Don't let the liquid simmer too hard or the chicken will be tough. Remove the pan from the heat, cover with a lid and let the chicken stand for 15 minutes to finish cooking. Cool the chicken then drain well, reserving the stock for another use. Using a large, sharp knife, cut the chicken into neat 5 mm (¼ inch) pieces. Place in a large bowl.

Meanwhile, steam the cauliflower over boiling water for 3–4 minutes or until tender, then remove to a colander to cool completely. Cut, if necessary, so it is roughly the same size as the chicken. Add to the chicken in the bowl and season with salt and pepper. Stir in the mayonnaise.

Spread half the bread slices with butter and then spread evenly with the filling. Top each with another slice of bread to make sandwiches. Using an electric knife, trim the crusts and then cut each sandwich into four neat triangles or fingers. Serve immediately.

Rich and filling, this makes a perfect meal for a winter's night; all it needs is plenty of decent bread, such as a good rye loaf, for dipping in. The only trick is not to let the soup simmer after you add the cheese or the soup will curdle. Not good.

CAULIFLOWER, CIDER AND CHEDDAR SOUP

Serves 6

3 tablespoons extra virgin olive oil
1 large onion, chopped
3 garlic cloves, chopped
900 g (2 lb/about 1 small-medium) cauliflower, trimmed and chopped
1 large carrot, chopped
1 celery stalk, chopped
2 x 330 ml (11¼ fl oz) bottles apple cider
1 liter (35 fl oz/4 cups) chicken stock, approximately
1 tablespoon Dijon mustard
200 g (7 oz) sharp cheddar cheese, grated
1 tablespoon cornstarch
Chopped chives and cayenne pepper, to serve

Heat the oil in a large saucepan over medium heat. Add the onion, garlic, cauliflower, carrot and celery and cover the pan. Cook, stirring often, for about 25 minutes or until the vegetables have softened. Add the cider and bring to a simmer, then add the stock and stir in the mustard.

Bring to a simmer then cook, uncovered, for 15 minutes or until the vegetables are very soft and starting to fall apart. Using an immersion blender or a food processor, process to a very smooth purée, adding a little extra stock if it is too thick. Bring the soup to a gentle simmer again.

Meanwhile, toss together the grated cheese and cornstarch in a bowl so the cheese is coated. Stirring constantly, add the cheese mixture to the soup and cook for 3–4 minutes or until the cheese melts and the soup thickens slightly—don't let it simmer or it will curdle. (If it does curdle, blend it with an immersion blender for several minutes; this will make it smooth.) Season the soup to taste with sea salt and freshly ground black pepper and serve sprinkled with chives and cayenne pepper.

A classic, elegant, puréed soup, this is the sort of dish that never goes out of fashion. The point of letting the vegetables cook in their own juices, rather than simply boiling them in the stock, is to extract maximum flavor. Cooked this way, they taste miraculously sweeter.

CAULIFLOWER SOUP WITH NUTMEG CREAM

Serves 4

1 tablespoon olive oil
1 tablespoon butter
1 leek, white part only, chopped
2 garlic cloves, chopped
5 sprigs of thyme
500 g (1 lb 2 oz/about ½ medium) cauliflower, trimmed and chopped
350 g (12 oz/about ½ large) celery root, peeled and chopped
560 ml (19¼ fl oz/2¼ cups) chicken stock, approximately
300 ml (10½ fl oz) half-and-half (18% fat)
1 tablespoon lemon juice, or to taste

NUTMEG CREAM
160 ml (5¼ fl oz) crème fraîche
1 teaspoon freshly grated nutmeg

For the nutmeg cream, combine the crème fraîche and grated nutmeg in a bowl, stir well and refrigerate.

Heat the oil and butter over medium heat in a large saucepan. Add the leek, garlic and thyme and cook, stirring often, for 5 minutes or until softened. Stir in the cauliflower and celery root. Cover the pan and cook, stirring often, for about 20 minutes or until the vegetables are tender—add a few tablespoons of water if they start to stick. Add the stock and bring to a simmer. Remove the thyme sprigs then, using an immersion blender or food processor, process to a smooth purée, adding a little extra stock if it is too thick. Return to the heat until nearly simmering. Stir in the half-and-half and lemon juice, season and serve with the nutmeg cream.

GOBI PARATHA

Makes 10 paratha

Cooks on the Indian subcontinent, where great swathes of the population are strict vegetarians, have many inspired ways to eat "gobi" (cauliflower). Here's a good one—a spicy cauliflower paste stuffed inside a warm flat bread.

500 g (1 lb 2 oz/about ½ medium) cauliflower,
    trimmed and chopped
2 tablespoons vegetable oil
1 teaspoon ground cumin
1½ teaspoons ground coriander
½ teaspoon ground turmeric
1 teaspoon chili powder, or to taste
1 teaspoon dried mango powder (amchur)
1 teaspoon salt
1 teaspoon freshly ground black pepper
Small handful of cilantro leaves,
    finely chopped
Indian lime pickles, to serve

PARATHA DOUGH
370 g (13 oz/2½ cups) whole-wheat flour
1½ teaspoons salt
2½ tablespoons vegetable oil
225 ml (7½ fl oz) warm water, approximately

CUMIN AND CARROT RAITA
1 tablespoon vegetable oil
1 onion, finely chopped
1 teaspoon cumin seeds
1 large carrot, grated
1 medium green chili, or to taste, sliced
375 ml (13 fl oz/1½ cups) Greek-style yogurt
1 teaspoon salt, or to taste
Handful of cilantro sprigs, chopped

For the paratha dough, combine the flour and salt in a bowl, then drizzle with the oil. Using your fingertips, work the oil into the flour. Add the water, a little at a time, until a soft dough forms, then knead for 5 minutes or until smooth. Cut the dough into 10 even pieces and roll each into a ball. Place the balls on a tray, cover with a damp cloth and leave for 30 minutes so the dough can relax.

For the cumin and carrot raita, heat the oil in a small saucepan, add the onion and cumin seeds and cook, stirring, for 5–6 minutes or until softened. Add the carrot and chili and cook, stirring, for 3–4 minutes or until the carrot softens. Remove from the heat and cool to room temperature. Stir together the yogurt, 2 tablespoons cold water, the salt and coriander in a bowl. Add the onion mixture and stir well, then refrigerate until required.

Working in batches, if necessary, place the cauliflower in a food processor and chop into small pieces—don't worry if there are a few lumps as it should have some texture. Heat the oil in a large frying pan over medium heat. Add the cauliflower, cover and cook, stirring often, for 5–6 minutes or until softened. Add the spices then cook, covered and stirring occasionally, for another 5 minutes or until the cauliflower is tender. Remove from the heat, stir in the salt and pepper and cool. Add the chopped cilantro.

Using a rolling pin and working with one ball at a time, roll out the dough on a lightly floured surface to a 12 cm (4½ inch) round. Place a heaped tablespoon of the filling in the middle, bring the edges together over the filling and pinch together firmly to seal. Flatten out the ball with your hand, seam side down, then roll out to about 12 cm (4½ inches) across. Take care as the filling can burst through, especially around the edges. (If it does, don't worry too much: you can still cook the paratha.)

Heat a large, heavy-based frying pan over medium heat. Cook the paratha, one at a time, for 3 minutes on each side or until cooked through, golden and slightly puffed. Serve hot, with raita and pickles.

Kick off an Italian-themed dinner party with this and you'll make friends for life. It's smooth, rich and cauliflowery in all the right places. Remember, you can use the chopped cauliflower core here as well as the florets—waste not, want not, and all of that.

CAULIFLOWER, BORLOTTI BEAN AND PANCETTA SOUP

Serves 4

2½ tablespoons extra virgin olive oil
150 g (5½ oz) piece of pancetta, cut into
    5 mm (¼ inch) pieces
2 garlic cloves, finely chopped
1 onion, finely chopped
2 sprigs of rosemary
800 g (1 lb 12 oz/about 1 small) cauliflower, trimmed
2 x 400 g (14-oz) cans borlotti beans
1 liter (35 fl oz/4 cups) chicken stock
125 ml (4 fl oz/½ cup) half-and-half (18% fat)

Heat 1 tablespoon oil in a large frying pan over medium–high heat. Add half the pancetta and cook, stirring often, for 8–10 minutes or until crisp. Transfer to a plate lined with paper towels and set aside.

Heat the remaining oil in a large saucepan over medium heat, add the remaining pancetta, garlic, onion and rosemary and cook, stirring often, for 5 minutes or until the onion is soft. Add the cauliflower then cover and cook, stirring often, for 20 minutes until tender. Add the borlotti beans and stock and bring to a simmer. Cook for 5 minutes then remove the rosemary. Using an immersion blender or food processor, process until smooth then add the half-and-half. Bring just to a simmer, then season to taste with sea salt and freshly ground black pepper. Ladle into bowls and top with the fried pancetta to serve.

SAL

Quick? Check. Easy? Check. Healthy? Check. Oh, and delicious too, let's not forget that. You could eat a bowl of this and call it dinner. But pair it with some grilled lamb, roast chicken or a whole steamed fish and crusty roast potatoes, and you've got a simply delicious feast.

CAULIFLOWER AND POMEGRANATE TABOULI

Serves 6 as a side

90 g (3¼ oz/½ cup) fine burghul (bulgur)
200 g (7 oz) small cauliflower florets
2 Lebanese (short) cucumbers, peeled and cut into
    5 mm (¼ inch) pieces
3 green onions (scallions), trimmed and very finely sliced
Handful of mint leaves, finely chopped
Large handful of flat-leaf parsley leaves, finely chopped
2–3 tablespoons lemon juice, to taste
4 tablespoons extra virgin olive oil
Seeds from 1 pomegranate

Rinse the burghul in a bowl of cold water, drain well then squeeze out the excess water with your hands. Using a food processor, finely chop the cauliflower until it resembles fine grains. Combine with the burghul in a large bowl, then add the cucumber, green onion, herbs, lemon juice, oil and pomegranate seeds, keeping a few tablespoons of the seeds to garnish. Toss well. Season to taste with sea salt and freshly ground black pepper and serve immediately, scattered with the pomegranate seeds.

It doesn't get much simpler than this dish—there's not even a moment of cooking involved. And it's flexible too—use hazelnuts if you prefer or just regular mozzarella if you can't find burrata. Your dish will still be great.

SHAVED CAULIFLOWER AND FENNEL SALAD WITH LEMON, ALMONDS AND BURRATA

Serves 6 as a side

80 g (2¾ oz/½ cup) almonds
500 g (1 lb 2 oz/about ½ medium) cauliflower, trimmed
2 baby fennel (about 400 g/14 oz), trimmed
Large handful of arugula or watercress sprigs
Handful of basil leaves, torn
250 g (9 oz) fresh burrata, torn into 2 cm (¾ inch) pieces

LEMON DRESSING
1 egg yolk
1 tablespoon Dijon mustard
1 tablespoon honey
3 teaspoons finely grated lemon zest
3 tablespoons lemon juice
150 ml (5 fl oz/generous ⅔ cup) olive oil

For the lemon dressing, combine the egg yolk, mustard, honey and zest in a large bowl. Whisk until smooth, then stir in the lemon juice. Whisking continuously, add the olive oil, a little at a time. Take care not to add the oil too quickly or the dressing will curdle. Continue adding the oil until a thick, emulsified dressing forms, then season to taste with sea salt and freshly ground black pepper.

Meanwhile, preheat the oven to 180°C (350°F). Place the almonds on a baking tray and roast for 15 minutes or until golden. Cool, then coarsely chop.

Using a very sharp large knife, slice the cauliflower through its stalk as thinly as you can. Cut the fennel bulbs in half lengthways and then slice as thinly as you can.

Mix the cauli and fennel in a large bowl with the arugula, basil and burrata and toss gently. Drizzle with the dressing and toss again. Scatter with the almonds to serve.

Salty, sour, spicy, fresh, crunchy—there's so much going on here, but somehow it all comes together in perfect harmony. Lentils are easy to cook, but have an annoying habit of overcooking right at the end. Keep your eye on them; you want them to have just a bit of bite but not lose their shape.

LENTIL, CAULIFLOWER AND WALNUT SALAD WITH POMEGRANATE MOLASSES DRESSING

Serves 4–6

80 g (2¾ oz/½ cup) walnuts
600 g (1 lb 5 oz/about ½ medium) cauliflower, trimmed and cut into florets
2½ tablespoons extra virgin olive oil
290 g (10¼ oz/1⅓ cups) brown lentils
90 g (3¼ oz/¾ cup) pitted green olives, cut in half lengthways
5 radishes, trimmed and thinly sliced
Large handful of watercress sprigs
Handful of mint leaves, coarsely chopped, or to taste
200 g (7 oz) feta, crumbled
Seeds from ½ pomegranate, to garnish
Mint leaves, to garnish

POMEGRANATE MOLASSES DRESSING

1½ teaspoons cumin seeds
2 garlic cloves, finely chopped
1½ tablespoons pomegranate molasses
2 teaspoons sugar
Large pinch of chili flakes, or to taste
250 ml (9 fl oz/1 cup) extra virgin olive oil
3 teaspoons lemon juice, or to taste

For the pomegranate molasses dressing, dry-fry the cumin seeds in a small, heavy-based frying pan over medium–low heat, shaking the pan often, for 2–3 minutes or until fragrant. Using a mortar and pestle or an electric spice grinder, grind or pound the seeds to form a coarse powder. Combine in a bowl with the garlic, pomegranate molasses, sugar and chili. Whisk until smooth then, continuously whisking, add the oil in a slow, steady stream. Whisk in the lemon juice. Add 2 tablespoons or so of boiling water if the mixture becomes very thick—some brands of pomegranate molasses will emulsify with the oil. Season with sea salt and black pepper.

Meanwhile, preheat the oven to 180°C (350°F). Roast the walnuts on a baking tray for about 8 minutes, then chop and set aside.

Place the cauliflower on a baking tray, drizzle with the olive oil and bake for 40 minutes or until tender and golden.

Cook the lentils in boiling water for 20–25 minutes or until tender but still holding their shape. Drain well and cool to room temperature.

Combine the lentils in a large bowl with the cauliflower, walnuts, olives, radish, watercress, chopped mint and feta. Drizzle with dressing and toss gently. Transfer to a platter and scatter with pomegranate seeds and mint leaves.

Throw some slices of fried firm tofu into this salad for a heartier effect. Fancy some meat in the mix? No worries, you can add some shredded poached chicken or cooked peeled shrimp. In either case, served with steamed jasmine rice this makes an excellent light summer dinner or lunch. A color hit of purple cauliflower would be excellent here.

THAI CAULIFLOWER AND EGG SALAD WITH A COCONUT-SWEET CHILI DRESSING

Serves 4

500 g (1 lb 2 oz/about ½ medium) cauliflower, trimmed and cut into small florets
270 g (9½ oz) snake (yard-long) beans or asparagus, trimmed and cut into 2.5 cm (1 inch) pieces
200 g (7 oz) bean sprouts
1 small red onion, very finely sliced
1–2 small red chilies, finely sliced, or to taste
Handful of cilantro sprigs
4 hard-boiled eggs, peeled and quartered
50 g (2 oz/⅓cup) unsalted roasted peanuts, chopped
2 tablespoons fried shallots, or to taste

COCONUT-SWEET CHILI DRESSING
4 cilantro roots, scrubbed and chopped
1 tablespoon shaved palm sugar
1 garlic clove, chopped
185 ml (6 fl oz/¾ cup) coconut cream
1½ tablespoons fish sauce
3 tablespoons sweet chili sauce
4 tablespoons fresh lime juice, or to taste
1½ teaspoons finely grated lime zest
2 tablespoons chopped cilantro

For the coconut-sweet chili dressing, mix the cilantro roots and palm sugar in a small food processor until the roots are finely chopped. Add all the remaining ingredients and process until smooth.

Steam the cauliflower over boiling water for 3 minutes or until nearly tender. Remove to a large bowl and cool.

Meanwhile, bring a pan of salted water to the boil. Add the beans and cook for 2 minutes, or until just softened. Transfer to a colander, reserving the cooking water, then cool under running water. Drain well. Lay out on a dish towel to absorb any liquid, then add to the cauliflower.

Add the bean sprouts to the boiling water, pressing down gently to submerge, then cook for about 2 minutes or just until they wilt. Transfer to a colander and cool under running water, drain well, then spread out on the dish towel. Add to the vegetables in the bowl with the onion, chili and cilantro sprigs.

Drizzle with dressing and toss gently. Season with sea salt and freshly ground black pepper and garnish with egg, peanuts and fried shallots.

The secret to making mayo is to have everything at room temperature when you start—including the egg yolks. Add the oil slowly: you can "break" the sauce if the oil goes in too fast and doesn't emulsify (you'll know if this ever happens—it will turn into a curdled mess). If it does "break," just start again using a fresh egg yolk and whisk the broken sauce very slowly into that.

CAULIFLOWER, CELERY ROOT AND APPLE REMOULADE

Serves 6 as a side

1 lemon, cut in half
400 g (14 oz/about ½ large) celery root
300 g (10½ oz) cauliflower, trimmed
1 Pink Lady, or other sweet, crisp apple
Large handful of flat-leaf parsley leaves, chopped
50 g (1¾ oz/¼ cup) drained baby capers
Crusty bread, to serve

HORSERADISH MAYONNAISE
2 egg yolks
2 tablespoons lemon juice, or to taste
3 tablespoons horseradish cream, or to taste
300 ml (10½ fl oz) olive oil

For the horseradish mayonnaise, combine the egg yolks, lemon juice and horseradish cream in a small food processor. With the motor running, add the olive oil, a little at a time, until the mixture begins to emulsify and thicken. Keep pouring the olive oil in a thin, steady stream, adding 1–2 tablespoons of warm water if the mixture becomes too thick—it should be creamy. Season the mayonnaise with salt and pepper to taste, adding a little more lemon juice or horseradish cream, if necessary. Transfer to a bowl and cover the surface with a piece of plastic wrap to prevent a skin forming.

Pour 1 liter (35 fl oz/4 cups) water into a large bowl and squeeze the juice of one of the lemon halves into it. Peel the celery root then, using a large, sharp knife, cut it into very fine matchsticks, placing them immediately into the acidulated water to prevent discoloration.

Trim the tough core from the cauliflower, then cut it into florets. Very finely slice the florets, lengthways.

Cut the apple in half, remove the core, slice the apple thinly and cut into fine matchsticks. Place in a bowl and toss with the juice from the remaining lemon half to prevent browning. Drain the celery root and pat dry with paper towels. Add to the apple with the cauliflower, parsley and capers. Add the mayonnaise and stir gently to coat everything. Season to taste with sea salt and freshly ground black pepper, then serve with crusty bread.

This is one of those easy salads—feel free to add more of one ingredient or less of something else. It won't be a flop if you don't have an avocado, so throw in some extra tomato instead, or if you use baby spinach leaves instead of the arugula. Za'atar is a Middle Eastern spice mix made of sesame seeds, oregano, thyme, savory and salt; it's delicious sprinkled over plain cooked vegetables. And freekah, another Middle Eastern ingredient, is made from wheat, picked when green and roasted to give a unique smoky flavor.

FREEKAH, CARROT, AVOCADO AND CAULIFLOWER SALAD WITH ZA'ATAR

Serves 4–6

800 g (1 lb 12 oz/about 1 small) cauliflower, trimmed and cut into small florets
2½ tablespoons extra virgin olive oil, plus extra for drizzling
2½ tablespoons za'atar, plus extra, to taste
180 g (6½ oz/1 cup) cracked freekah, rinsed well
2 carrots
1 large ripe avocado, thinly sliced
2 roma (plum) tomatoes, cut into 1 cm (½ inch) pieces
85 g (3 oz/½ cup) Sicilian (Nocellara) olives
Handful of baby arugula leaves
Juice of 1 lemon

Preheat the oven to 180°C (350°F). Place the cauliflower on a large baking tray, drizzle with olive oil, then bake for 25 minutes or until light golden. Sprinkle with the za'atar and bake for another 5–10 minutes or until tender.

Meanwhile, put the freekah and 750 ml (26 fl oz/ 3 cups) water in a saucepan, bring to a simmer, then cover with a lid. Cook over medium–low heat for about 25 minutes or until the freekah is tender and the water absorbed. Meanwhile, peel the carrots then cut into long, fine ribbons with the peeler. When the freekah is cooked, remove from the heat, stir in the carrot, then cover and leave for about 10 minutes or until the carrot is wilted. Transfer to a large bowl and cool.

Add the cauliflower, avocado, tomatoes, olives and arugula leaves to the bowl and toss gently. Drizzle with lemon juice and olive oil, then season with sea salt and freshly ground black pepper. Serve scattered with za'atar.

Skordalia, a Greek dip-spread-sauce, generally fashioned out of potato, almonds and plenty of garlic, packs a punch. It's not for anyone who is shy of garlic, but if you love it, you've come to the right place. As for the vegetables here, you can steam or chargrill them if you prefer instead of roasting. Throw in a few handfuls of broad beans or sugar snaps, some thin wedges of fennel or whatever you fancy that's green and in season. The skordalia also works with medium-rare roast lamb, grilled salmon or even a steak.

ROASTED SPRING GREENS WITH CAULIFLOWER SKORDALIA

Serves 4–6

300 g (10½ oz) asparagus, trimmed
400 g (14 oz) green beans, trimmed
360 g (13 oz) broccolini, trimmed
2½ tablespoons extra virgin olive oil
4 hard-boiled eggs, peeled and halved
100 g (3½ oz) dried black or kalamata olives
Ciabatta or other rustic bread, to serve

CAULIFLOWER SKORDALIA
250 g (9 oz/about 1 large) all-purpose potato, peeled and cut into 2.5 cm (1 inch) pieces
250 g (9 oz) small cauliflower florets
5 garlic cloves, coarsely chopped
160 ml (5¼ fl oz/generous ¾ cup) extra virgin olive oil
2 tablespoons lemon juice, or to taste

For the cauliflower skordalia, cook the potato in boiling, salted water for 12 minutes or until tender. Drain well, then push through a potato ricer into a bowl.

Meanwhile, steam the cauliflower over boiling water for 6 minutes or until very tender. Transfer to a colander and cool. Mix the cauliflower, garlic and oil in a food processor to a smooth purée. Stir into the potato with the lemon juice and season well with sea salt and freshly ground black pepper, adding a little extra lemon juice if necessary.

Preheat the oven to 180°C (350°F). Spread the vegetables over two baking trays in a single layer and drizzle with the olive oil. Roast for 30 minutes until the vegetables are tender and light golden. Arrange on a platter with the eggs, scatter with olives and season to taste with sea salt and freshly ground black pepper. Serve with the skordalia and slices of ciabatta.

This is from the Moroccan culinary repertoire, where smashed/mashed vegetable salads are commonplace. They're called "zahlouk" and eggplant is generally used, but cauliflower tastes just great. Use chopped green beans in place of the zucchini if you like and add some dried black olives for an extra, tangy deliciousness.

SMASHED CAULIFLOWER AND CHICKPEA SALAD WITH HARISSA DRESSING

Serves 4-6

600 g (1 lb 5 oz/about ½ medium) cauliflower, trimmed and cut into small florets
300 g (10½ oz/about 2) zucchini, finely diced
1 x 400 g (14-oz) can chickpeas, drained and rinsed
2½ tablespoons drained baby capers
½ preserved lemon, pulp discarded, rinsed and chopped
Handful of flat-leaf parsley leaves, chopped

HARISSA DRESSING
2½ tablespoons harissa, or to taste
2 garlic cloves, very finely chopped
1 teaspoon caraway seeds
Juice of 1 lemon, or to taste
170 ml (5½ fl oz/⅔ cup) olive oil

For the harissa dressing, whisk the harissa, garlic, caraway seeds and lemon juice until smooth. Whisking continuously, add the olive oil in a thin, steady stream, then season to taste with sea salt and freshly ground black pepper.

Steam the cauliflower over boiling water for 6–7 minutes or until nearly tender, then add the zucchini and cook for another 4 minutes or until the vegetables are very tender. Remove to a bowl and cool. Add the chickpeas and roughly mash with a potato masher. Stir in the capers, preserved lemon, parsley and harissa dressing. Season to taste with sea salt and freshly ground black pepper and a little extra lemon juice, or harissa, to taste.

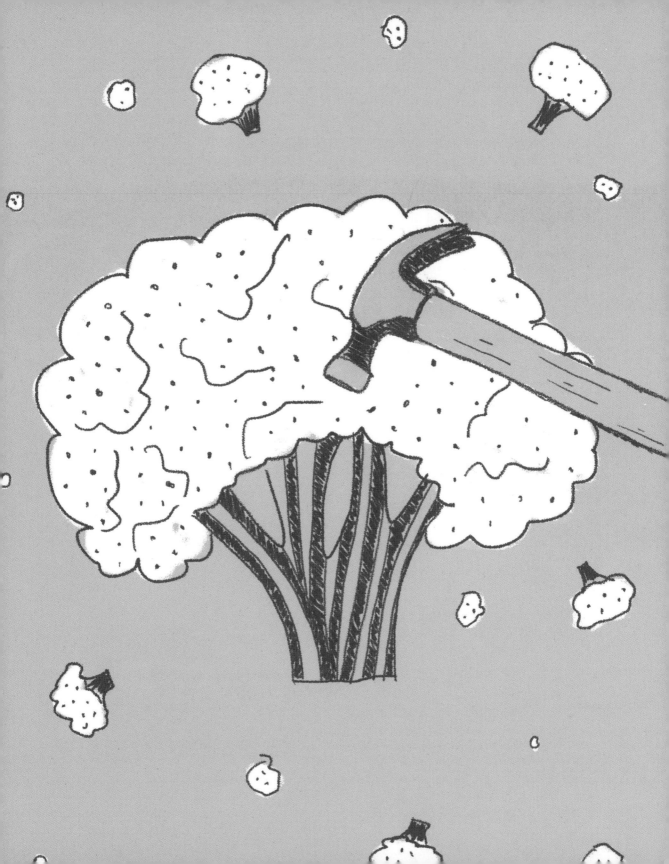

Close relatives, broccoli and cauli go perfectly together and chargrilling brings out their earthy sweetness. Purple cauliflower looks particularly good here. Dukkah, an Egyptian condiment, has become ubiquitous. You can buy it at the supermarket, but it's so much fresher tasting when you make your own—and you can season it how you like. The recipe here makes around a cup of dukkah; you won't need that much for the recipe, but it's a pain to make in smaller quantities. Keep it in an airtight container for a month or so and you can use it on other salads, or as a dip for bread with olive oil.

CHARRED CAULIFLOWER AND BROCCOLI SALAD WITH PISTACHIO DUKKAH

Serves 4–6

600 g (1 lb 5 oz/about ½ medium) cauliflower
600 g (1 lb 5 oz) broccoli
4 tablespoons extra virgin olive oil
Lemon wedges, to serve

PISTACHIO DUKKAH
50 g (1¾ oz/⅓ cup) sesame seeds
80 g (2¾ oz/generous ½ cup) pistachio nuts
1 tablespoon cumin seeds
1 tablespoon coriander seeds
1½ teaspoons sea salt flakes, or to taste
1 teaspoon freshly ground black pepper, or to taste

For the pistachio dukkah, preheat the oven to 180°C (350°F). Place the sesame seeds and pistachios on separate baking trays. Roast the sesame seeds for 8–10 minutes or until deep golden. Roast the pistachios for 6 minutes or until light golden. Cool.

Meanwhile, heat a small, heavy-based frying pan over medium–low heat. Add the cumin and coriander seeds and dry roast, shaking the pan often, for 3–4 minutes until fragrant. Transfer to a spice grinder or mortar and pestle and grind coarsely. Transfer to a food processor, add the sesame seeds, pistachios, salt and pepper and process until the pistachios are finely chopped but with a little texture.

Trim the cauliflower and broccoli, taking care to leave plenty of stalk intact. Cut each into large florets, then cut each floret down the middle into medium-sized pieces. Combine in a large bowl with the oil, tossing to coat well. Heat a grill pan or barbecue to medium high. Grill the florets, in batches if necessary and turning occasionally, for 6–7 minutes or until charred and tender. Transfer to a platter, scatter with dukkah to taste, then serve with lemon wedges for squeezing.

MAKE
MEA
IT

A
OF

This salady type of meal is big on texture and flavor. Serve this on brown rice to make it even more healthy. There are lots of different types of miso; shiro miso is pale, slightly sweet and contains half the salt of most other varieties. Find the pickled daikon in any Japanese or good Asian food store—they're generally a yellow color.

MISO-GLAZED CAULIFLOWER BOWL

Serves 4

330 g (11½ oz/1½ cups) medium-grain rice
350 g (12 oz/6 cups) frozen podded edamame, thawed
5 radishes, trimmed and thinly sliced
1 carrot, trimmed and cut into very fine matchsticks
400 g (14 oz) skinless, boneless salmon,
    cut into 5 mm (¼ inch) pieces
100 g (3½ oz) Japanese pickled daikon, thinly sliced
Shredded nori, to serve
1 tablespoon toasted sesame seeds, to serve
Lime wedges and tamari soy sauce, to serve

MISO-GLAZED CAULIFLOWER
500 g (1 lb 2 oz/about ½ medium) cauliflower, trimmed
1 teaspoon finely grated fresh ginger
2 tablespoons shiro miso
1 tablespoon rice bran oil or any neutral-tasting
    vegetable oil
1 tablespoon sesame oil
1 tablespoon rice wine vinegar
2 tablespoons mirin

For the miso-glazed cauliflower, preheat the oven to 180°C (350°F). Cut the cauliflower into small florets and place in a baking dish in a single layer. Combine the remaining ingredients in a small food processor and process until smooth. Pour over the cauliflower in the dish and toss to coat well. Bake for about 35 minutes, stirring occasionally, or until the cauliflower is golden and cooked through.

Meanwhile, combine the rice and 560 ml (19¼ fl oz/ 2¼ cups) water in a saucepan and bring to the boil. Cover the pan and cook over medium–low heat for 12 minutes or until the water is absorbed. Remove from the heat and stand, covered, for 5 minutes for the rice to finish cooking.

Cook the edamame in boiling, salted water for 5 minutes or until tender, then drain well.

Spoon the rice into four bowls, then arrange the edamame, radish, carrot, salmon and pickles around the edge in neat piles. Scatter the nori over the salmon. Spoon the miso-glazed cauliflower into the middle of each bowl and scatter with sesame seeds. Serve with lime wedges for squeezing and some soy sauce for dipping.

This is one of those really simple dishes that appears almost artless; however, the layers of flavor and texture at play make it anything but. Buy decent sourdough for the crumbs, get the freshest shrimp you can lay your hands on and use homemade chicken stock, if that's practical. Orecchiette, by the way, is a rustic dried pasta from Puglia in Italy's south; its shape is said to resemble little ear lobes, which is what the name means.

ORECCHIETTE WITH CAULIFLOWER, SHRIMP AND CHILI CRUMBS

Serves 4

225 g (8 oz) sourdough bread, crusts removed
125 ml (4 fl oz/½ cup) extra virgin olive oil
1 teaspoon chili flakes, or to taste
600 g (1 lb 5 oz/about ½ medium) cauliflower,
    trimmed and cut into 1 cm (½ inch) pieces
4 garlic cloves, thinly sliced
350 g (12 oz) orecchiette
185 ml (6 fl oz/¾ cup) chicken stock
600 g (1 lb 5 oz) raw king shrimp,
    peeled, cleaned and halved lengthways
Handful of flat-leaf parsley leaves, chopped
Salad leaves and lemon wedges, to serve

Preheat the oven to 180°C (350°F).

Tear the bread into pieces, place in a food processor, then process until large crumbs form—take care not to overprocess as they should have plenty of texture. Spread in a baking dish, drizzle with half the olive oil, sprinkle with the chili flakes and toss to coat. Bake for 15 minutes or until golden and very crisp.

Heat the remaining oil in a large, deep, non-stick frying pan over medium heat. Add the cauliflower and garlic, cover and cook, stirring occasionally, for 12 minutes or until golden.

While the cauliflower cooks, bring a large saucepan of salted water to the boil. Add the orecchiette and cook for 15 minutes, or according to the packet, until al dente.

Add the stock and shrimp to the cauliflower, increase the heat to medium–high, cover, then cook, stirring occasionally, for 5 minutes or until the shrimp are cooked through. Season to taste with sea salt and freshly ground black pepper. Toss with the parsley and drained pasta. Divide into bowls, scatter with the chili crumbs, then serve with salad leaves and lemon wedges.

Taleggio is a washed-rind cheese from northern Italy and although it has a pronounced pong its flavor is surprisingly sweet and mild. Creamy and melty, it's lovely here with the cauliflower, rice and nuts, but you could use a blue cheese, such as gorgonzola dolce, instead.

CAULIFLOWER, TALEGGIO AND HAZELNUT RISOTTO WITH BURNT BUTTER

Serves 4

50 g (1¾ oz/⅓ cup) hazelnuts
2 tablespoons extra virgin olive oil
100 g (3½ oz/⅓ cup) butter
1 onion, finely chopped
2 garlic cloves
500 g (1 lb 2 oz/about ½ medium) cauliflower,
    trimmed and cut into florets
300 g (10½ oz/1⅓ cups) arborio or other risotto rice
125 ml (4 fl oz/½ cup) white wine
1.25 liters (44 fl oz/5 cups) simmering chicken or
    vegetable stock, approximately
200 g (7 oz) taleggio, chopped
12 sage leaves

Heat the oven to 180°C (350°F). Place the hazelnuts on a small tray and roast for 10 minutes or until light golden. Wrap the nuts in a dish towel, then leave for 5 minutes to allow the skins to loosen. Rub the nuts in the towel to remove the skins. Coarsely chop the nuts and set aside.

Heat the oil and 2 tablespoons of the butter in a large saucepan over medium heat. Add the onion and garlic then cook, stirring, for 6 minutes or until the onion has softened.

Add the cauliflower, cover the pan and cook, stirring occasionally, for 8 minutes or until softened. Stir in the rice and cook, stirring, for 2 minutes or until heated through. Add the wine, bring to the boil and cook, stirring, until the wine has nearly evaporated.

Add about 250 ml (9 fl oz/1 cup) of the hot stock then cook, stirring constantly, until the stock is nearly all absorbed. Add another 250 ml (9 fl oz/1 cup) of stock and stir until nearly absorbed. Repeat until the stock has gone and the rice is just cooked through; the mixture should be very creamy—add a little extra stock, or water, if necessary. Stir in the taleggio, season to taste with sea salt and freshly ground pepper and cover to keep the risotto warm.

Heat the remaining butter in a frying pan over medium–high heat, add the sage leaves and cook, swirling the pan occasionally, for 2–3 minutes, or until the butter smells nutty. Add the hazelnuts. Divide the risotto into four bowls, then spoon butter mixture over each bowl and serve.

Really, you can never have too many cheesy, pasta-y, cauliflower-filled bakes in your repertoire and this one, with its crunchy topping, is a winner. Use whatever short pasta shape you like—fusilli or spirali, for instance, would be perfect.

CRUNCHY CAULIFLOWER PENNE BAKE

Serves 6

800 g (1 lb 12 oz/about 1 small) cauliflower, trimmed and cut into small florets
3 tablespoons extra virgin olive oil
175 g (6 oz) penne
50 g (1¾ oz/¼ cup) butter
1 onion, finely chopped
2 garlic cloves, finely chopped
40 g (1½ oz/generous ¼ cup) plain (all-purpose) flour
1 liter (35 fl oz/4 cups) milk, heated
75 g (2½ oz/½ cup) chopped sun-dried tomatoes
6 anchovy fillets, chopped
50 g (1¾ oz/¼ cup) drained baby capers
100 g (3½ oz/¾ cup) grated mozzarella cheese
80 g (2¾ oz/1 cup) finely grated parmesan cheese
Large handful of basil leaves, chopped
Large handful of flat-leaf parsley leaves, chopped

TOPPING

4 x 1.5 cm (⅝ inch) slices of day-old sourdough bread
2½ tablespoons extra virgin olive oil
80 g (2¾ oz/¾ cup) grated parmesan cheese

Preheat the oven to 180° C (350°F). Spread the cauliflower on a large baking tray, drizzle with 2 tablespoons of the olive oil and bake for 30 minutes or until golden and tender.

Meanwhile, cook the penne in boiling, salted water for 10 minutes or according to packet instructions, until al dente. Drain well then set aside.

Heat the remaining oil and butter in a saucepan over medium heat. Add the onion and garlic and cook, stirring often, for 6–7 minutes or until the onion is tender. Add the flour and stir well, reducing the heat to medium–low. Stirring constantly to prevent lumps forming, add the milk, ½ cup (125 ml/4 fl oz) at a time, allowing it to come to a simmer before adding more. Cook the sauce, stirring often, for 6–7 minutes. Remove from the heat, stir in the sun-dried tomatoes, anchovies and capers, then the cheeses and herbs. Season to taste with sea salt and freshly ground black pepper. Arrange the pasta in a large baking dish, scatter with cauliflower and pour the sauce over the top.

For the topping, remove the crusts from the bread and cut into 1.5 cm (⅝ inch) cubes. Toss with the olive oil and scatter over the pasta. Sprinkle with parmesan and bake for 40 minutes or until the topping is golden and crisp and the sauce is bubbling.

Basmati rice looks different, smells different and cooks different to other rices, so don't use any other variety here. When it's tender, the characteristically long, slender, elegant grains should be quite dry and separate—never gluggy. This dish makes a great vegetarian weekend dinner—scatter with some boiled egg wedges if you want to amp up the protein. And really, use whatever Indian chutney or relish you prefer or serve a selection.

CASHEW AND CAULIFLOWER BIRYANI

Serves 6

300 g (10½ oz/1½ cups) basmati rice
3 tablespoons ghee
2 large onions, thinly sliced
4 garlic cloves, finely chopped
½ star anise
6 cardamom pods, crushed
1 cinnamon stick
1 tablespoon garam masala
8 whole cloves
1 bay leaf
700 ml (24 fl oz/3 cups) chicken stock or water
800 g (1 lb 12 oz/about 1 small) cauliflower, trimmed and cut into medium florets
235 g (8½ oz/1½ cups) toasted unsalted cashews, very coarsely chopped
Large handful of cilantro sprigs, chopped
Naan bread, Indian eggplant chutney and Greek-style yogurt, to serve

Rinse the rice under cold running water then drain well. Heat the ghee in a saucepan over medium heat, add the onion and garlic and cook, stirring, for 5–6 minutes or until softened.

Add all the spices and bay leaf and cook, stirring, for 2–3 minutes until fragrant. Add the rice, stir to coat, then add the stock, cauliflower and cashews. Bring to a simmer, cover tightly and cook over medium–low heat for 12 minutes or until the liquid has been absorbed.

Remove from the heat and leave for 3 minutes for the rice to finish cooking. Serve, scattered with cilantro and with naan bread, chutney and yogurt passed around separately.

Serve these for brunch or as a light, easy weekend dinner. If you are looking for a gluten-free scenario, then just use your favorite commercial gluten-free flour instead of the plain wheat flour.

CAULIFLOWER AND PECORINO FRITTERS WITH BAKED PEARS

Serves 4

500 g (1 lb 2 oz/about ½ medium) cauliflower, trimmed
50 g (1¾ oz/⅓ cup) plain (all-purpose) flour
1 teaspoon baking powder
1 teaspoon salt
1 teaspoon freshly ground black pepper
½ teaspoon freshly ground nutmeg
5 large eggs, lightly beaten
100 g (3½ oz/1 cup) grated pecorino cheese
Olive oil, for cooking
Arugula leaves, to serve
Prosciutto, to serve

BAKED PEARS
2 large firm pears, cut into quarters and cored
3 teaspoons balsamic vinegar
1½ tablespoons extra virgin olive oil
4 sprigs of thyme
1½ teaspoons sugar

For the baked pears, preheat the oven to 180°C (350°F). Place the pear quarters in a single layer in a baking dish then drizzle with vinegar and oil. Scatter with thyme and sugar, then bake for 50 minutes, turning occasionally, or until the pears are golden and very tender. Reduce the oven temperature to 120°C (235°F).

Meanwhile, cut the cauliflower into small pieces (about 1 cm/½ inch) and steam over boiling water for 3–4 minutes until tender. Remove from the heat, transfer to a colander and cool. Transfer to a large bowl and sprinkle with the flour, baking powder, salt, pepper and nutmeg. Stir well to coat the cauliflower. Add the egg and pecorino and mix well.

Heat a few tablespoons of oil over medium heat in a large, non-stick frying pan. Add half cupfuls of mixture to the pan spreading them a little with a spatula to form pancakes about 11 cm (4¼ inches) across. Cook for 4 minutes on each side or until deep golden, slightly puffy and cooked through. Transfer to a plate, cover loosely with foil and keep warm in the oven while you cook the rest. Serve with arugula leaves, prosciutto and roasted pears.

It's been said before but it's a drum worth beating: homemade curry paste tastes way better than anything you'll ever buy. You just can't get those same snappy flavors unless you grind the ingredients fresh, and it's really easy too. Truthfully, the food processor does all the work for you. Plus, you can make double the recipe and freeze the extra for another time. It will keep in an airtight container in the freezer for 5–6 weeks.

THAI YELLOW CAULIFLOWER, SNAKE BEAN <u>AND</u> TOFU CURRY

Serves 4

2 tablespoons peanut oil
1 onion, finely chopped
400 g (14 oz/about ½ small) cauliflower, trimmed
    and cut into medium–large florets
375 ml (13 fl oz/1½ cups) chicken stock
200 g (7 oz) snake (yard-long) beans, trimmed and
    cut into 3 cm (1¼ inch) pieces
140 g (5 oz/1 cup) frozen or fresh podded peas
400 g (14 oz) fried tofu puffs, sliced
1 x 400 ml (14-fl oz) can coconut cream
Steamed jasmine rice, to serve
70 g (2½ oz/½ cup) unsalted roasted peanuts
Large handful of Thai basil leaves
2 kaffir lime leaves, stems removed, finely shredded
Lime wedges, to serve

YELLOW CURRY PASTE
1½ tablespoons chopped fresh ginger
2 lemongrass stems, white part only, chopped
5 garlic cloves, chopped
1½ teaspoons ground turmeric
3 Asian shallots, chopped
5 large kaffir lime leaves, stems removed, chopped
4 small red chilies, chopped
1 tablespoon fish sauce
1½ tablespoons vegetable oil

For the yellow curry paste, mix all the ingredients in a small food processor to a smooth paste. Alternatively, pound everything, except the fish sauce and oil, with a mortar and pestle. then stir in the fish sauce and oil.

Heat the oil in a large pan over medium heat. Add the onion and cook, stirring, for 5 minutes until softened. Add the curry paste and cook, stirring, for 3 minutes or until fragrant. Add the cauliflower, stir to coat, then add the stock; the cauliflower won't quite be covered. Place the beans and peas on top and add the tofu, but do not stir. Bring the stock to a simmer, cover the pan tightly, then cook over medium heat for 12–15 minutes until the vegetables are just tender; they should still have a little bite.

Add the coconut cream, season with sea salt and freshly ground black pepper and bring to a simmer. Cook for 3 minutes or until heated through, then divide into bowls with steamed rice. Scatter with peanuts, basil and the shredded lime leaves. Serve with lime wedges.

Roll up, roll up, cauli-loving carnivores—is this a deal for you! Classic mac and cheese amped up with bacon AND pepperoni, rounded out with sweet nuggets of cauliflower. Of course, those who prefer can ditch the meat for a completely vegetarian-friendly version.

MEAT-LOVERS' CAULIFLOWER MAC 'N' CHEESE

Serves 6

600 g (1 lb 5 oz/about ½ medium) cauliflower, trimmed and cut into 1.5 cm (⅝ inch) pieces
2½ tablespoons olive oil
175 g (6 oz) rindless bacon, chopped
60 g (2¼ oz/¼ cup) butter
60 g (2¼ oz/generous ⅓ cup) plain (all-purpose) flour
750 ml (26 fl oz/3 cups) milk, heated
200 g (7 oz/2 cups) grated cheddar cheese
200 g (7 oz/1¼ cups) macaroni
100 g (3½ oz) thinly sliced pepperoni

Preheat the oven to 200°C (400°F).

Place the cauliflower in a large, deep ovenproof frying pan 35 cm (14 inches) wide and drizzle with olive oil. Bake for 25 minutes until light golden, then scatter with the bacon. Bake for 20 minutes or until the bacon is cooked through.

Meanwhile, melt the butter in a large saucepan over medium heat. Add the flour and stir until a thick, smooth paste forms. Stirring constantly with a whisk to prevent lumps forming, add the milk, 125 ml (4 fl oz/½ cup) or so

at a time, bringing the mixture to a simmer before adding any more. Once all the milk is added, cook over low heat for 6–7 minutes, whisking occasionally to prevent lumps. Season to taste and stir in half the cheese.

Meanwhile, bring a large saucepan of salted water to the boil. Add the macaroni and cook for 8 minutes, or according to packet directions, until al dente. Drain well.

Combine the macaroni with the cauliflower mixture in the pan and then pour over the sauce. Scatter with the remaining cheese then place the pepperoni slices over the top in neat rows. Bake for 25 minutes or until hot and bubbling. Serve immediately.

Kedgeree is from the Anglo-Indian school of cookery, popularised in Victorian England by colonials returning home after a stint in the subcontinent. Its origins are thought to lie in an Indian, spice-infused, lentil and rice dish called khichari. In England it became a fashionable brunch, featuring smoked haddock and enriched with cream. Here's a non-traditional version, healthier through the addition of plenty of cauliflower.

CAULIFLOWER AND SMOKED FISH KEDGEREE

Serves 4

1 hot smoked baby trout (about 400 g/14 oz)
2 tablespoons vegetable oil
2 tablespoons butter
1 onion, chopped
600 g (1 lb 5 oz/about ½ medium) cauliflower,
    trimmed and cut into medium florets
2 bay leaves
2 garlic cloves, chopped
1½ tablespoons finely chopped fresh ginger
2 tablespoons curry powder, or to taste
300 g (10½ oz/1½ cups) basmati rice
580 ml (20 fl oz/2⅓ cups) chicken stock or water
1 teaspoon sea salt, or to taste
4 hard-boiled eggs, peeled and cut into quarters
Handful of flat-leaf parsley, coarsely chopped
Lime quarters, to serve
Sweet mango chutney, to serve

Remove the flesh from the trout, discarding the skin and bones. Break the flesh into large pieces and refrigerate until needed.

Heat the oil and butter in a large, deep frying pan over medium heat. Add the onion and cauliflower and cook for 8–10 minutes, stirring often, until the cauliflower is beginning to brown. Add the bay leaves, garlic and ginger and cook, stirring, for 2 minutes or until fragrant. Add the curry powder and cook for 1 minute until fragrant. Sprinkle the rice over the top in an even layer, add the stock and salt and bring to a simmer. Cover tightly and cook over medium–low heat for 12 minutes or until the liquid is absorbed.

Remove the pan from the heat, quickly scatter the trout and egg quarters over the top, then replace the lid and leave the kedgeree for 10 minutes to allow the rice to finish cooking and the fish and egg to heat through.

Season the kedgeree with freshly ground black pepper, scatter with parsley and serve with lime quarters and sweet mango chutney.

This is a cheat's paella—the real deal is cooked in open, shallow pans over a fire fueled by orange and pine wood and pine cones. This is said to impart a characteristic smokiness, called a "paellera," to the dish, which diners then eat directly out of the pan. So, now you know why we are cheating here.

SMOKY SHRIMP, CHORIZO AND CAULIFLOWER PAELLA

Serves 4

2½ tablespoons olive oil
1 large onion, finely chopped
2 garlic cloves
350 g (12 oz/about 3) firm chorizo sausages, sliced
2½ teaspoons smoked paprika
½ teaspoon saffron threads (optional)
300 g (10½ oz/1½ cups) long-grain rice
625 ml (21 fl oz/2½ cups) chicken stock
1 x 400 g (14-oz) can chopped tomatoes
500 g (1 lb 2 oz/about ½ medium) cauliflower, trimmed and cut into large florets
140 g (5 oz/1 cup) frozen peas
300 g (10½ oz) raw king or tiger shrimp, peeled and cleaned
Large handful of cilantro, chopped

Heat the olive oil in a large, deep, heavy-based pan over medium heat. Add the onion and garlic and cook, stirring, for 5 minutes or until softened.

Add the chorizo, paprika and saffron, if using, and cook, stirring, for another 3–4 minutes or until some of the fat renders out of the chorizo and the spices are fragrant. Stir in the rice, then add the stock and tomatoes and bring to a simmer. Scatter with the cauliflower and peas, cover the pan then simmer for 15–17 minutes or until the rice is nearly tender.

Stir in the shrimp, cover the pan, then remove from the heat and leave for 7 minutes or until the shrimp are cooked and the rice is tender. Season to taste with sea salt and freshly ground black pepper, then stir in the cilantro.

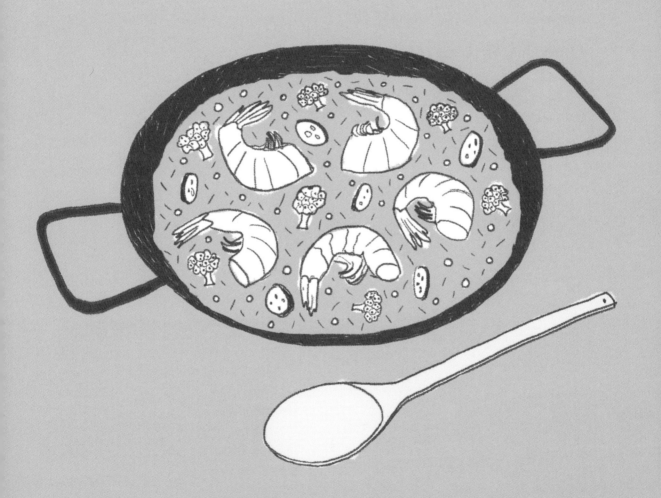

Taking inspiration from classic Lebanese flavors, this dish is seriously simple. You literally bake everything together in dishes, then drizzle over an easy tahini sauce, scatter with arugula and pine nuts and voila—dinner sorted.

BAKED CHICKEN AND CAULIFLOWER WITH TAHINI

Serves 4

50 g (1¾ oz/⅓ cup) pine nuts
600 g (1 lb 5 oz/about ½ medium) cauliflower, trimmed and cut into large florets
600 g (1 lb 5 oz/about 3) red-skinned or other all-purpose potatoes, peeled and cut into 3 cm (1¼ inch) pieces
Olive oil, for drizzling
Large handful of baby arugula
Pita bread, to serve
Chopped flat-leaf parsley and lemon wedges, to serve

MARINATED CHICKEN

4 chicken leg quarters
4 garlic cloves, very finely chopped
Juice of 1 lemon
1 teaspoon ground cinnamon
1 teaspoon ground allspice
1 teaspoon freshly ground black pepper
1 teaspoon salt
2½ tablespoons olive oil

TAHINI SAUCE

4 garlic cloves, chopped
180 g (6½ oz/⅔ cup) tahini
100 ml (3½ fl oz) Greek-style yogurt
3 tablespoons lemon juice

For the marinated chicken, use a large, sharp knife to cut each chicken quarter in half through the thigh joint. Trim the spine edge of the thigh and trim the knuckle at the end of each drumstick. Combine the remaining ingredients in a large bowl and stir to combine well. Add the chicken and turn to coat well. Cover the bowl with plastic wrap then refrigerate for 2 hours or overnight.

For the tahini sauce, mix the garlic, tahini, yogurt and lemon juice in a food processor until smooth. Add 80 ml (2½ fl oz/⅓ cup) water and process to a creamy sauce, adding more water if needed. Season with sea salt and pepper and refrigerate until needed.

Preheat the oven to 180°C (350°F). Toast the pine nuts for 7–8 minutes until golden, then set aside to cool.

Divide the chicken, cauliflower and potato into two baking dishes and season well with salt and pepper. Drizzle generously with olive oil, then roast for 40 minutes or until the vegetables and chicken are golden and cooked through, swapping the trays halfway through. Scatter with arugula and pine nuts, drizzle with the tahini sauce and serve with pita bread, a sprinkling of parsley and the lemon wedges.

Miso is big on flavor and good for you too, delivering a dose of protein, vitamins and minerals. Made by fermenting soy beans, it has a nutty sweetness that complements cauliflower, and other vegetables, perfectly. Even if you're not vegetarian, this hearty stew will soon become a go-to cool weather staple. Shichimi togarashi is a Japanese seasoning mix, available from Asian or specialist Japanese food stores.

CAULIFLOWER, KALE, WHITE BEAN AND MISO HOTPOT

Serves 4

235 g (8½ oz/1¼ cups) dried white beans
2 tablespoons peanut oil
1 onion, chopped
2 garlic cloves, chopped
2 tablespoons finely chopped fresh ginger
200 g (7 oz/about 1 large) red-skinned or other all-purpose potato, cut into chunks
300 g (10½ oz/about 2) carrots, cut into chunks
6 kale leaves, stems discarded, torn
400 g (14 oz/about ½ small) cauliflower
1 liter (35 fl oz/4 cups) chicken stock
125 ml (4 fl oz/½ cup) cooking sake
100 g (3½ oz) shiro miso
1 tablespoon sesame oil
Shichimi togarashi (Japanese 7-spice powder), to serve
Steamed brown rice, to serve

Soak the beans in cold water overnight then drain well. Put in a saucepan, cover with cold water, then bring to a simmer, skimming off any foam. Cook over medium heat for about 35 minutes or until tender. Drain well.

Meanwhile, heat the oil in a large saucepan over medium heat, add the onion, garlic and ginger and cook, stirring, for 5 minutes or until softened. Stir in the potato and carrot, cover the pan and cook, stirring occasionally, for 10 minutes or until beginning to soften. Add the kale, cauliflower, stock and cooking sake, pushing the vegetables to submerge. Bring to a simmer, cover and cook for 10–15 minutes or until all the vegetables are tender.

Using a ladle, remove about 250ml (9 fl oz/1 cup) of the hot cooking liquid to a bowl. Add the miso, whisk until smooth, then add to the pan with the cooked beans and sesame oil. Season to taste, sprinkle with shichimi togarashi to taste and serve with steamed brown rice.

Curried cauliflower is a no brainer: the vegetable king goes so well with Indian spices. Paneer is the cheese of choice in India and Pakistan—a mellow, fresh, curd-style cheese that takes on other flavors well and doesn't melt when heated. You can buy it from Indian food stores.

CAULIFLOWER, PANEER AND PEA CURRY

Serves 4

4 tablespoons ghee
1 large onion, finely chopped
4 garlic cloves, finely chopped
2 tablespoons finely chopped fresh ginger
800 g (1 lb 12 oz/about 1 small) cauliflower, trimmed and cut into small florets
355 g (12½ oz/2½ cups) thawed frozen or podded fresh peas
1 teaspoon ground turmeric
2 teaspoons ground coriander
2 teaspoons ground cumin
1 teaspoon Kashmiri chili powder, or to taste
4 cardamom pods, crushed
500 ml (17 fl oz/2 cups) vegetable stock
3 tomatoes, cut into 2 cm (¾ inch) pieces
300 g (10½ oz) paneer, cut into 1.5 cm (⅝ inch) pieces
2½ tablespoons lime, juice, or to taste
Steamed basmati rice, to serve

Heat the ghee in a large saucepan over medium heat. Add the onion, garlic and ginger and cook, stirring, for 5 minutes or until the onion is tender. Add the cauliflower, peas and spices and cook, stirring, for 3 minutes or until fragrant.

Add the stock and bring to a simmer. Cover and cook over medium–low heat for 5 minutes, then stir in the tomato and paneer.

Cover the pan and cook for about 10 minutes or until the vegetables are tender. Season to taste, then add the lime juice. Serve with basmati rice.

Here's a play on those classic southern Italian sweet-and-sour flavors—anchovies, garlic, raisins, pine nuts and vinegar. By the time everything has finished cooking this delicious combo has so transformed the cauli that it barely tastes like its unadorned self. The secret is in the long, slow cooking—this is not a dish to rush.

PASTA WITH PAN-ROASTED CAULIFLOWER, RAISINS AND ANCHOVIES

Serves 4

100 ml (3½ fl oz) extra virgin olive oil
900 g (2 lb/about 1 small–medium) cauliflower, trimmed and cut into 2 cm (¾ inch) pieces
3 garlic cloves, thinly sliced
6 anchovy fillets, chopped
45 g (1½ oz/¼ cup) raisins, coarsely chopped
400 g (14 oz) dried fettuccine or linguine
2½ tablespoons pine nuts, toasted (optional)
2 tablespoons balsamic vinegar, or to taste
250 ml (9 fl oz/1 cup) chicken stock
Handful of flat-leaf parsley, chopped
Grated pecorino or parmesan cheese, to serve

Heat the oil over medium heat in a large, deep frying pan, add the cauliflower and garlic and cook, stirring often, for 20 minutes or until the cauliflower is softened and golden. Stir in the anchovies and raisins and continue cooking, stirring often, for another 15–20 minutes, or until the cauliflower is almost collapsing and light golden— add 1–2 tablespoons of water to the pan if the mixture starts to stick.

When the sauce mixture is almost cooked, bring a large saucepan of salted water to the boil and cook the pasta for 10 minutes, or according to the packet, until al dente, then drain well. Add the pine nuts, balsamic vinegar, stock and parsley to the cauliflower mixture and bring to a simmer. Season to taste, then spoon the pasta into bowls, top each with cauliflower sauce and scatter with pecorino.

CAULI TACOS

Makes 12 tacos

If you don't want to deep-fry, no worries... Spread the cauli on a paper-lined tray and spray with olive oil; bake in a 190°C (375°F) oven for 30 minutes for crisp cauli that's lower in fat and delicious. (Arguably, not QUITE as delicious, but it's your call.) You'll need a tortilla press here.

270 g (9½ oz) masa harina
800 g (1 lb 12 oz/about 1 small) cauliflower, trimmed
2 eggs, beaten well
150 g (5½ oz/1 cup) plain (all-purpose) flour
1½ teaspoons chili powder
1½ teaspoons cumin seeds
2 teaspoons dried oregano
1½ teaspoons salt
1 teaspoon freshly ground black pepper
Vegetable oil, for deep-frying

GUACAMOLE
2 ripe avocados
2 garlic cloves
2 tablespoons lime juice, or to taste

RED CABBAGE SLAW
½ small red cabbage, trimmed, cored and finely shredded
1 carrot, very finely shredded
Handful of cilantro, chopped
170 ml (5½ fl oz/⅔ cup) whole-egg mayonnaise

For the tacos, combine the masa harina with 300 ml (10½ fl oz) water in a bowl and using a fork, mix to combine until a soft, pliable dough forms. Add a little more masa harina if it is too soft, or more water if too firm. Divide the dough into 12 even pieces and roll each into a ball. Open your tortilla press and cover the base with parchment paper. Place a ball in the centre and cover with another sheet of parchment paper. Firmly close the tortilla press then open, turn the taco in the paper 180 degrees and gently press again to make an even thickness. Peel off the top layer of paper, turn the taco over and carefully peel away the other layer of paper. Place on a parchment paper-lined tray and repeat with the remaining dough.

Heat a frying pan over medium heat and cook the tacos, in batches, for 1 minute on each side or until cooked through. Transfer to a plate and cover with a damp dish towel to keep them soft and pliable.

For the guacamole, combine all the ingredients in a food processor, season well with salt and pepper and process until smooth, adding a little extra lime juice if necessary.

For the red cabbage slaw, mix all the ingredients in a bowl until the vegetables are coated with mayonnaise. Add more mayonnaise to taste and season well.

Preheat the oven to 120°C (235°F).

Cut the cauliflower into 1 cm (½ inch) pieces. Whisk the egg and 1 tablespoon water in a bowl. Mix together the flour, spices, oregano, salt and pepper in another bowl.

Heat about 6 cm (2½ inches) of oil, or enough to deep-fry, in a large saucepan to 160°C (315°F) or until a cube of bread turns golden in 60 seconds. Working in batches, toss the cauliflower in the egg mixture to coat well, allowing excess to drain off. Toss to coat in the flour mixture, shaking off any excess flour. Deep-fry the cauliflower, in batches, for 7–8 minutes or until tender, crisp and golden. Keep warm in the oven on a plate lined with paper towel while you cook the remaining cauliflower.

To serve, fill each taco with some coleslaw, guacamole and fried cauliflower.

A tagine is a cooking vessel used in Morocco and Algeria, as well as being the name of the various slow-cooked, stew-like dishes that are made in it. Tagines feature lots of lively flavors from traditional ingredients such as spices, sweet fruit and honey, meats, vegetables and preserved lemon.

MOROCCAN BEEF TAGINE WITH DATES AND CAULIFLOWER

Serves 4

80 ml (2½ fl oz/⅓ cup) extra virgin olive oil
3 small onions, cut into thick wedges
1 tablespoon ras el hanout, or to taste
1.2 kg (2 lb 10 oz) beef chuck steak, or other
    braising cut, trimmed
500 ml (17 fl oz/2 cups) beef stock
2½ tablespoons honey
500 g (1 lb 2 oz/about ½ medium) cauliflower,
    trimmed and cut into florets
300 g (10½ oz) fresh dates, pitted
85 g (3 oz/⅔ cup) pitted green olives
1 preserved lemon, pulp discarded, rinsed and chopped
Large handful of cilantro sprigs, chopped
Harissa and couscous, to serve

Heat half the oil in a large, deep frying pan over medium heat. Add the onion and cook, turning often, for 8 minutes or until golden. Add the ras el hanout and stir well.

Meanwhile, cut the beef into large pieces, about 3 cm (1¼ inches) across. Heat the remaining oil in a large, heavy-based frying pan over medium–high heat, add the beef, in batches if necessary, and season to taste. Cook, turning, for 5 minutes or until browned all over. Add to the onion in the pan, with any cooking juices, the stock and honey. Bring to a simmer, then cover tightly and cook over low heat for 45 minutes or until the beef is nearly tender. Add the cauliflower, dates and olives, cover and cook for 15 minutes or until the cauliflower is cooked and the beef is very tender. Scatter with preserved lemon and cilantro, then serve with couscous and harissa.

GOCHUJANG CAULI LETTUCE WRAPS

Serves 4

Wrapping morsels in lettuce is a popular way to dine in Korea and is great for informal entertaining. Gochujang is a fermented savory/spicy condiment made from glutinous rice with a sweet edge; buy it from Korean grocers and it will keep for a few months in the fridge.

900 g (2 lb/about 1 small–medium) cauliflower, trimmed and cut into florets
Vegetable oil, for deep-frying
Sesame seeds, for sprinkling
200 g (7 oz) firm tofu, sliced
Large oak leaf, or other soft lettuce
Steamed rice, to serve

SEASONED SPINACH

240 g (8½ oz) baby spinach leaves, washed
2 garlic cloves, finely chopped
3 teaspoons soy sauce
2½ teaspoons sesame seeds
3 teaspoons sesame oil

SEASONED BEAN SPROUTS

350 g (12 oz) bean sprouts
2 green onions (scallions), trimmed and very finely sliced
1 tablespoon toasted sesame seeds
3 teaspoons clear rice vinegar, or to taste
1 tablespoon sesame oil

GOCHUJANG SAUCE

100 g (3½ oz/⅓ cup) gochujang (Korean spice paste)
110 g (3¾ oz/½ cup) sugar
4 garlic cloves, very finely chopped
2 tablespoons rice vinegar
2 tablespoons mirin

CAULIFLOWER BATTER

110 g (3¾ oz/¾ cup) plain (all-purpose) flour
30 g (1 oz/¼ cup) potato starch
30 g (1 oz/¼ cup) cornstarch
200 ml (7 fl oz) iced water, approximately

For the seasoned spinach, put the spinach in a large pan over medium–high heat, cover and cook for 2–3 minutes, shaking the pan, until just wilted. Transfer to a colander, run under cold water to cool it down, then drain well. Using your hands, gather the spinach into a ball and squeeze out as much liquid as possible. Whisk together the remaining ingredients in a bowl, add the spinach and toss to coat. Season with salt and pepper.

For the seasoned bean sprouts, bring a pan of salted water to the boil, add the sprouts and cook for 2–3 minutes until wilted. Transfer to a colander, drain, then cool under running water. Spread out on a layer of paper towel, with more towel on top, then press gently to soak up as much liquid as possible. Whisk together the remaining ingredients. Add the sprouts and toss to coat.

For the gochujang sauce, combine the gochujang, sugar, garlic, vinegar, mirin and 170 ml (5½ fl oz/⅔ cup) water in a saucepan and whisk well. Bring to a simmer then cook, stirring occasionally, over medium–low heat for about 10 minutes or until reduced and thickened to a coating consistency. Remove from the heat.

For the cauliflower batter, whisk together the flour, potato starch, cornstarch and about 175 ml (6 fl oz/¾ cup) of the iced water until smooth. Add enough of the remaining water to form a creamy batter with a light, coating consistency.

Heat enough oil for deep-frying in a wok or large, deep saucepan to 170°C (340°F) or until a cube of bread turns golden in 50 seconds. Working in batches, dip the cauliflower in the batter, allowing excess to drain off. Deep-fry the cauliflower for 7–8 minutes until the coating is crisp and the cauliflower tender. Transfer to a plate lined with paper towel to drain.

Toss the cauliflower in the gochujang, transfer to a warm platter and scatter with sesame seeds. Serve with the tofu, seasoned veggies, lettuce for wrapping, and steamed rice.

This Turkish-inspired dish stands up well to being fiddled around with. For instance, instead of the pastirma (spicy, dry-cured beef), stir just-steamed fresh mussel meat or cooked shrimp into the finished pilaf. Or stir cubes of lamb rump into the burghul, adding them with the cauliflower.

SPICED CAULIFLOWER, SPINACH AND PASTIRMA PILAF WITH GOLDEN ONIONS

Serves 4–6

80 ml (2½ fl oz/⅓ cup) extra virgin olive oil
1 large onion, finely chopped
3 garlic cloves, finely chopped
1 teaspoon ground allspice
1½ teaspoons sweet paprika
1½ tablespoons tomato paste (concentrated purée)
1 cinnamon stick
55 g (2 oz/⅓ cup) currants
50 g (1¾ oz/⅓ cup) pine nuts
265 g (9¼ oz/1½ cups) coarse burghul (bulgur)
580 ml (20¼ fl oz/2⅓ cups) chicken stock
600 g (1 lb 5 oz/about ½ medium) cauliflower, trimmed and cut into large florets
120 g (4¼ oz) baby spinach
200 g (7 oz) thin slices pastirma, torn
Handful of dill, chopped
Greek-style yogurt and lemon wedges, to serve

GOLDEN ONIONS
4 tablespoons extra virgin olive oil
3 large onions, thinly sliced

Heat the olive oil in a large, heavy-based sauté pan or large saucepan over medium heat. Add the onion and garlic and cook, stirring, for 5–6 minutes or until softened. Add the allspice, paprika and tomato paste and cook, stirring, for 1 minute or until fragrant. Add the cinnamon stick, currants, pine nuts and burghul and stir well. Add the stock, bring to the boil, cover the pan and cook for 5 minutes.

Working quickly, scatter the cauliflower into the pan, season to taste, then cover and cook for 10 minutes or until the liquid has been absorbed and the burghul and cauliflower are tender. Try not to lift the lid while the pilaf is cooking. Stir in the spinach then remove from the heat and leave, covered, for 5 minutes or until the spinach wilts. Stir in the pastirma and dill.

Meanwhile, make the golden onions. Heat the oil in large, heavy-based frying pan over medium heat and cook the onions, stirring, for 20 minutes or until deep golden. Scatter over the cooked pilaf and serve with the Greek yogurt and lemon wedges.

This lemon sauce is from the Greek avgolemono school of saucery, where stock is thickened a little using egg yolk and flour. It's spiked with lemon juice and zest. The flour, as well as thickening, stabilizes the mixture so the egg yolks don't curdle when the sauce simmers.

CAULIFLOWER AND LAMB MEATBALLS IN LEMON SAUCE

Serves 4

100 g (3½ oz/scant ½ cup) medium-grain rice
250 g (9 oz) cauliflower, trimmed and chopped
350 g (12 oz) minced (ground) lamb
1½ teaspoons ground cumin
Handful of flat-leaf parsley, finely chopped
1 egg, beaten well
1 teaspoon salt
1 teaspoon freshly ground black pepper
1.25 liters (44 fl oz/5 cups) chicken stock

AVGOLEMONO
2 tablespoons plain (all-purpose) flour
2 egg yolks
2 teaspoons finely grated lemon zest
4 tablespoons lemon juice

Soak the rice in boiling water for 10 minutes, then drain well. Meanwhile, place the cauliflower in a food processor and process until it resembles rice. Remove to a bowl with the drained rice, minced lamb, cumin, parsley, egg and salt and pepper. Take heaped teaspoonfuls of the mixture and roll into balls with your hands.

Bring the chicken stock to a simmer in a large saucepan. Lower the meatballs into the stock, taking care not to break them up. Bring to a very gentle simmer and cook over medium–low heat for 20 minutes or until the meatballs are cooked and the rice is tender. Using a slotted spoon, remove the meatballs from the stock.

For the avgolemono, whisk the flour, egg yolks, lemon zest and juice in a bowl until smooth. Take a cupful of hot stock from the pan and whisk it into the lemon mixture then, whisking constantly, add it back to the pan. Whisk the liquid in the pan for about 5 minutes until it comes to a simmer and thickens slightly. Return the meatballs to the sauce to gently heat through.

Kids love these and adults do too. They're meaty yet lean, flavorsome and healthy and are enough to fill you up for dinner. Try to get your hands on decent sourdough buns with plenty of good chew, although by all means use whatever type of bun is your favorite. It's hardly make-or-break.

CHICKEN AND CAULIFLOWER BURGERS WITH ROAST TOMATOES AND PESTO

Serves 4

500 g (1 lb 2 oz/about ½ medium) cauliflower, trimmed and cut into small florets
100 ml (3½ fl oz) extra virgin olive oil
3 large firm, ripe tomatoes, cut into wedges
1½ tablespoons balsamic vinegar
1½ teaspoons sugar
500 g (1 lb 2 oz) minced (ground) chicken
60 g (2¼ oz/1 cup) fresh breadcrumbs
1 egg yolk
1 teaspoon sea salt
1 teaspoon freshly ground black pepper
4 sourdough hamburger buns, split
80 ml (2½ fl oz/⅓ cup) whole-egg mayonnaise
1 firm, ripe avocado, sliced
Handful of baby arugula leaves

PESTO
1 garlic clove, chopped
50 g (1¾ oz/⅓ cup) pine nuts
50 g (1¾ oz/½ cup) grated parmesan cheese
2 large handfuls of basil leaves
125 ml (4 fl oz/½ cup) extra virgin olive oil

For the pesto, mix all the ingredients in a food processor to a coarse paste. Season with salt and pepper, then transfer to a small bowl. Cover the surface with plastic wrap to prevent it discoloring.

Preheat the oven to 180°C (350°F). Place the cauliflower in a single layer on a baking tray and drizzle with 2½ tablespoons of the olive oil. Roast for 35 minutes or until golden and tender, then cool.

Meanwhile, arrange the tomato in a single layer in a baking dish. Drizzle with 2 tablespoons of the remaining oil and the balsamic, sprinkle with sugar, then season with sea salt and pepper. Bake for 40 minutes or until light golden.

Place the cauliflower in a bowl and break it up with your hands. Add the minced chicken, breadcrumbs, egg yolk, salt and pepper and mix well. Divide into four even portions and shape each into a patty about 10 cm (4 inches) across.

Heat the remaining oil in a large, non-stick frying pan and cook for 15 minutes over medium heat, turning once, or until deep golden and cooked through.

While the patties are cooking, preheat the grill and toast the buns until golden on both sides. Spread the bottom half with mayonnaise and top with a patty. Top with tomato, avocado slices and arugula, then spoon on some pesto. Pop the tops on the buns and serve immediately.

Think of this Iranian staple as a herb-laden frittata. In traditional recipes the quantity of herbs used outweighs the amount of egg, which is merely there to bind everything together. The cooked kuku is served with vegetable pickles, bread and yogurt, sometimes with walnuts used to garnish.

CAULIFLOWER, TURMERIC AND HERBS KUKU

Serves 4–6

1 large handful of cilantro
1 large handful of flat-leaf parsley
1 large handful of dill
2 large handfuls of baby spinach, arugula
    or watercress sprigs
4 tablespoons extra virgin olive oil
1 onion, finely chopped
2 garlic cloves, finely chopped
400 g (14 oz/about ½ small) cauliflower,
    trimmed and finely chopped
1½ teaspoons ground turmeric
100 g (3½ oz/⅔ cup) dried barberries or currants
8 eggs, beaten well
1 tablespoon plain (all-purpose) flour
½ teaspoon baking powder
1 teaspoon salt
1 teaspoon freshly ground black pepper

Wash all the herbs and the spinach leaves and shake dry. Spin in a salad spinner to remove as much water as possible, or pat dry with paper towels. Chop finely: there should be about five packed cupfuls of greens.

Heat half the oil in a large saucepan over medium heat. Add the onion, garlic and cauliflower and cook, stirring often, for 12–15 minutes or until the vegetables are soft. Stir in the turmeric and barberries and cook for another 1–2 minutes or until fragrant. Add the chopped greens and cook, stirring, for 5 minutes or until they are completely wilted. Remove from the heat and cool slightly.

Preheat your grill to medium–high.

Whisk together the eggs, flour, baking powder and salt and pepper in a large bowl then stir in the herb mixture. Heat a non-stick 21 cm (8¼ inch) frying pan with an ovenproof handle over medium heat. Pour in the egg mixture, reduce the heat slightly and cook for 6 minutes or until the base has set. Using a spatula, push the edge of the kuku into the middle of the pan, so the uncooked mixture runs to the sides. Cook for another 5–6 minutes or until the edges are cooked and the middle is beginning to set, then put under the grill for 6–7 minutes until deep golden and cooked through. Serve hot or at room temperature, cut into wedges.

This celebratory one-pan dish is Palestinian and, although the prep might seem daunting, once it's all done the recipe is a breeze. Even if the finished thing falls apart a bit (or a lot!) when you turn it out, no worries: it will still taste great. If you're too chicken to turn it out, you can always serve directly from the pan. Baharat is an aromatic spice mix that you can buy from spice shops or Middle Eastern grocers.

MAQLUBA

Serves 6

800 g (1 lb 12 oz/about 1 small) cauliflower, trimmed and cut into florets
Olive oil, for cooking
2 large eggplants (about 950 g/2 lb 2 oz)
335 g (12 oz/1⅔ cups) basmati rice
1 kg (2 lb 4 oz) lamb forequarter chops, trimmed and cut into 2–3 cm (¾–1¼ inch) pieces
1 large onion, finely chopped
4 garlic cloves, chopped
5 teaspoons baharat
½ teaspoon saffron threads (optional)
55 g (2 oz/⅓ cup) currants
50 g (1¾ oz/⅓ cup) pine nuts
2 bay leaves
750 ml (26 fl oz/3 cups) chicken stock, approximately
1 teaspoon freshly ground black pepper
1½ teaspoons sea salt
4 large roma (plum) tomatoes, thinly sliced
Greek yogurt and chopped cilantro, to serve

Preheat the oven to 180°C (350°F). Spread the cauliflower over a large baking tray or dish, drizzle generously with olive oil and bake for 35 minutes or until golden.

Cut the eggplant into 1 cm (½ inch) thick slices and layer in a large colander, sprinkling each layer lightly with salt as you go. Leave for 30 minutes or until the eggplant has given up some of its juices. Rinse well, drain, then dry on paper towels. Place the eggplant in a single layer on two baking trays. Drizzle with oil and bake for 25 minutes until tender.

While the eggplant is cooking, soak the rice in warm water for 30 minutes, then drain well.

Heat 1½ tablespoons of oil in a large, heavy-based frying pan over medium–high heat. Add the lamb and cook, turning, for 2–3 minutes until browned. Remove to a bowl.

Heat 2½ tablespoons of oil in a pan over medium heat, add the onion and garlic and cook, stirring, for 5 minutes until soft. Add the spices, currants, pine nuts and bay leaves and cook, stirring, for 1–2 minutes until fragrant. Add the stock, pepper and salt and bring to a simmer. Cover and keep hot.

Lightly oil the base of a 24 cm (9½ inch) wide and 10 cm (4 inch) deep pan. Layer the eggplant neatly in the base, overlapping slightly. Scatter with two thirds of the rice, then pour in half the hot stock mixture. Scatter the cauliflower in an even layer and arrange the lamb in an even layer over the top, adding any juices from the meat. Scatter with the remaining rice, pour on the remaining stock and lay the tomato over the top. Press the mixture down to ensure it's even and compact. Add extra stock or water to just cover the rice, if necessary.

Place the pan over medium–high heat and cook until the stock starts to simmer. Cover with a tight-fitting lid, then reduce the heat to low and cook, without uncovering, for 30 minutes until the liquid is absorbed. Remove from the heat and leave for 10 minutes, covered. Turn out onto a large platter, scatter with cilantro and serve with yogurt.

Utterly delicious though traditional lasagne is, it's not quick to make and excludes vegetarians with its minced meat sauce. Here's an alternative that's lighter, chock-full of vegetables and far less taxing on the cook than the original classic.

CAULIFLOWER, CELERY ROOT AND PUMPKIN LASAGNE

Serves 6

400 g (14 oz/about ½ small) cauliflower, coarsely chopped
500 g (1 lb 2 oz) celery root, trimmed, peeled and thinly sliced
300 ml (10½ fl oz) milk
300 ml (10½ fl oz) half-and-half (18% fat)
300 g (10½ oz/1⅓ cups) firm, fresh ricotta cheese
Handful of basil leaves, chopped
½ teaspoon freshly ground nutmeg
200 g (7 oz/2 cups) grated parmesan cheese
1 kg (2 lb 4 oz) Japanese pumpkin (kabocha), peeled and
    cut into 4 cm (1½ inch) pieces
3 zucchini, cut lengthways into
    5 mm (¼ inch) slices
150 g (5½ oz) instant lasagne sheets
Arugula salad and crusty bread, to serve

Preheat the oven to 180°C (350°F) and lightly grease a 2 liter (70 fl oz/8 cup) baking dish.

Process the cauliflower in a food processor until very finely chopped. Set aside.

Place the celery root, milk and half-and-half in a saucepan and add enough water to just cover the celery root. Bring to a simmer, cover the pan and cook for 15 minutes over medium–low heat or until the celery root is very tender.

Drain, reserving 300 ml (10½ fl oz) of the cooking liquid. Combine the celery root and reserved liquid in a food processor and process until smooth. Add the ricotta, basil, nutmeg and half the parmesan, season to taste with sea salt and freshly ground black pepper and process to combine well.

Spread about 5 tablespoons of the celery root mixture in the dish. Scatter with a quarter of the cauliflower, then about a third of the pumpkin and zucchini, seasoning each layer as you go. Spread a layer of lasagne sheets over the top. Spread with about 5 tablespoons more of the celery root mixture, then continue layering until everything is used up, finishing with a layer of celery root mixture and cauliflower. Scatter with the remaining parmesan and cover with foil.

Bake for 30 minutes, then remove the foil and bake for another 30 minutes until golden and cooked through. Serve with a arugula salad and crusty bread.

There's nothing technically difficult about cutting "steaks" from cauliflower, but in order for them to hold together you've got to include the core in each slice. What this means is that there will be quite a bit that won't make the cut, so just use that for another recipe. Stored in a zip lock bag in the fridge, offcuts will keep for 4–5 days. Oh, and here are two sauces for serving with your steaks—hot bacon or an Italian salsa verde. Your call.

CAULIFLOWER STEAKS, TWO WAYS

Serves 4

1 small cauliflower, trimmed
Olive oil, for cooking

SALSA VERDE
60 g (2¼ oz/1 cup very tightly packed) curly parsley
Large handful of mint leaves
2 garlic cloves, chopped
1 hard-boiled egg yolk
1½ tablespoons lemon juice, or to taste
3 teaspoons grain mustard
¼ small onion, chopped
6 anchovy fillets
2½ tablespoons drained baby capers
125 ml (4 fl oz/½ cup) extra virgin olive oil

HOT BACON DRESSING
1 tablespoon olive oil
200 g (7 oz) rindless smoky bacon, finely sliced
1 tablespoon Dijon mustard
4 tablespoons cider vinegar
1½ teaspoons cornstarch

To make the salsa verde, mix all the ingredients to a coarse paste in a food processor. Add a little extra lemon juice, if required, and season well with sea salt and freshly ground black pepper.

For the hot bacon dressing, heat the olive oil in a frying pan over medium heat and cook the bacon, stirring, for 20 minutes or until deep golden and the fat has rendered out. Keeping the pan on the heat, whisk in the mustard, vinegar and 230 ml (7¾ fl oz/scant 1 cup) water until smooth. Mix 1 tablespoon water with the cornstarch to form a smooth paste. Bring the liquid in the pan to a simmer then add the cornstarch, stirring constantly, until it simmers and thickens.

Preheat the oven to 180°C (350°F).

Cut the cauliflower in half widthways, then cut two 2 cm (¾ inch) thick slices from each half, through the core. Use the remaining ends of the cauliflower for something else— for the steaks, you want the middle section with the core intact, which holds the slices together. Drizzle with oil and grill or chargrill, in batches, for 7 minutes each side, then transfer to the oven and cook for 10–12 minutes more until the cores are tender.

Serve the steaks hot with either salsa verde or hot bacon dressing (if the bacon dressing has thickened on standing, stir in 1–2 tablespoons of boiling water to thin it).

BAK
CAU

THAT

For the best results, use a very firm and dry feta, drained well of any residual brine. Spreading the cauliflower mixture over the tray is a less sticky proposition if you spray your hands with oil first. Serve these with your favorite Mediterranean-style dip—hummus or baba ghanoush, for example. Oh, and drinks . . . don't forget the drinks!

CAULIFLOWER, FETA AND SUNFLOWER NIBBLES

Makes 24 nibbles

80 g (6½ oz) cauliflower florets
130 g (4½ oz/1 cup) grated firm dry feta
95 g (3¼ oz/½ cup) lentil flour
1 teaspoon baking powder
1 teaspoon freshly ground black pepper
1 teaspoon sea salt
55 g (2 oz/⅓ cup) sunflower seeds
2 eggs, beaten well
3 tablespoons extra virgin olive oil

Preheat the oven to 170°C (340°F). Line a 32 cm (12½ inch) square baking tray with parchment paper.

Place the cauliflower in a food processor and finely chop. Transfer to a dish towel and, using your hands, wring out as much liquid as possible. Tip into a bowl with the remaining ingredients, stirring with a fork to mix well.

Using your hands, spread the mixture evenly over the tray so it covers it completely. Bake for about 50 minutes, turning the tray occasionally so the mixture cooks evenly, or until deep golden. While still hot, cut into 24 pieces and transfer to a wire rack to cool. If the nibbles soften too much, stick them back in a 160°C (320°F) oven for about 10 minutes until crisp.

Not all pizza involves tomato sauce, but by all means spread your favorite variety over the uncooked bases (before everything else goes on). Sometimes, though, simplicity can't be improved on—this pizza is a delicious case in point.

CAULIFLOWER-BOCCONCINI PIZZA BIANCA

Serves 4

400 g (14 oz/about ½ small) cauliflower, trimmed, leaving the core intact
8 mozzarella bocconcini balls (about 250 g/9 oz), sliced
80 g (2¾ oz/¾ cup) grated parmesan cheese
2 teaspoons chili flakes, or to taste
4 tablespoons extra virgin olive oil
Handful of basil leaves

PIZZA BASE
250 ml (9 fl oz/1 cup) lukewarm water
Large pinch of sugar
2 teaspoons instant dried yeast
200 g (7 oz/1⅓ cups) plain (all-purpose) flour
150 g (5½ oz/1 cup) whole-wheat flour
1½ teaspoons salt
2 tablespoons olive oil

For the pizza base, combine the water and sugar in an electric mixer. Sprinkle with the yeast and leave for 5 minutes or until the yeast is foamy. Add the flours, salt and olive oil then, using the dough hook, mix for 8 minutes or until a smooth, soft, elastic dough forms. Alternatively, you can mix the dough with a wooden spoon then turn it out onto a lightly floured board and knead for 7–8 minutes, taking care not to incorporate too much extra flour—the dough should be slightly sticky. Place the dough in a lightly oiled bowl, turn it to coat, then cover the bowl tightly with plastic wrap. Leave in a draught-free place for about 45 minutes or until it has doubled in size.

Preheat the oven to 250°C (500°F) or as high as it will go. Lightly flour two pizza or baking trays.

While the dough is rising, cut the cauliflower in half down the middle, then cut each half into neat slices about 5 mm (¼ inch) thick, breaking or cutting any large slices in two down the middle. Place the cauliflower slices in a saucepan with 125 ml (4 fl oz/½ cup) water, cover the pan and bring to a simmer over medium–high heat. Cook for 3–4 minutes or until nearly tender, then drain in a colander, taking care not to break the cauliflower slices.

Using your hand, deflate the pizza dough, then turn it out onto a lightly floured surface. Cut the dough in half, then form each into a neat ball. On a lightly floured surface and using a lightly floured rolling pin, roll each round out to around 28 cm (11¼ inches) across. Place each round on a baking tray and top with the cauliflower slices and cheese. Scatter with chili flakes and season well. Drizzle with the olive oil and bake for 12–15 minutes, switching the trays halfway through, until bubbling on top and the bases are golden and crisp. Scatter with basil and serve immediately.

These are good to pass around with drinks, with their salty, cheesy tang and herby freshness. You can roll the pastries 2–3 hours in advance and refrigerate them until you're ready to bake. Buy your filo from the refrigerator section of the supermarket, not the freezer, as thawed frozen sheets can be brittle and difficult to work with.

CAULIFLOWER, POTATO AND FETA BOREK

Makes 24 borek

350 g (12 oz/about 2) red-skinned or other all-purpose
    potatoes, peeled and cut into 2.5 cm (1 inch) pieces
2½ tablespoons extra virgin olive oil
400 g (14 oz/about ½ small) cauliflower, trimmed
    and cut into 1 cm (½ inch) pieces
2 garlic cloves, finely chopped
½ teaspoon ground allspice
150 g (5½ oz) feta cheese, finely crumbled
Small handful of mint leaves, chopped
Small handful of flat-leaf parsley leaves, chopped
1 egg, beaten well
375 g (13 oz) filo pastry
175 g (6 oz) unsalted butter, melted and cooled
1 egg yolk
Nigella seeds, for sprinkling

Cook the potato in boiling, salted water for 8 minutes or until tender. Drain well.

Meanwhile, heat the oil in a saucepan over medium heat, add the cauliflower and garlic, then cover the pan and cook, stirring occasionally, for 15 minutes or until the cauliflower is very tender. If it threatens to stick, add 1–2 tablespoons of water. Remove from the heat, add the potato then, using a potato masher, mash together to form a coarse purée. Cool slightly.

Stir the allspice, feta and herbs into the cauliflower mixture, then season to taste and stir in the egg.

Preheat the oven to 180°C (350°F) and line a large baking tray with parchment paper.

Lay the filo sheets on the bench and cover with a damp dish towel to prevent drying out. Place 1 sheet of pastry on a board and brush it lightly all over with melted butter. Place another sheet on top and brush with butter; repeat with another sheet so you have a stack of three layers. Cut the pastry into quarters.

Working with one piece of pastry at a time, brush around the edges lightly with butter, then place 1 tablespoon of the potato mixture along a long edge of the pastry, forming it into a log about 8 cm (3¼ inches) long. Fold the two sides of pastry over the filling and brush with butter. Roll the pastry up to form a neat log. Repeat with the remaining pastry, butter and filling, placing the borek on the tray.

Stir the egg yolk in a bowl with 1 tablespoon water. Brush over the top of each borek, then sprinkle lightly with nigella seeds. Bake for 20–25 minutes or until golden and crisp.

Whoever came up with this idea is a genius; a completely wheat- and gluten-free pizza base, with cauliflower picking up the slack. While there are any number of variations on this theme, not all recipes take you down the squeezing-the-cauliflower route, which is critical for the firm base. You really do need to squeeze, and squeeze hard.

CAULIFLOWER CRUST PIZZA

Serves 4

400 g (14 oz) cherry tomatoes, halved
24 pitted kalamata olives
100 ml (3½ fl oz) extra virgin olive oil
200 ml (7 fl oz) tomato passata (puréed tomatoes)
250 g (9 oz/2 cups) grated mozzarella cheese
100 g (3½ oz/1 cup) grated parmesan cheese
Large handful of basil leaves

PIZZA BASE
900 g (2 lb/about 1 small–medium) cauliflower, trimmed
1 x 400 g (14-oz) can white beans, drained well
2 eggs
1½ teaspoons salt
1 teaspoon freshly ground black pepper

For the pizza base, cut the cauliflower into pieces then, working in batches, mix in a food processor until very finely chopped and resembling rice. Combine the cauliflower in a large saucepan with 125 ml (4 fl oz/½ cup) water and cover tightly with a lid. Place over medium–high heat and cook, stirring often, for 4–5 minutes or until tender. Remove to a colander lined with a dish towel then cool slightly.

Preheat the oven to 180°C (350°F) and line two baking trays with parchment paper.

When the cauliflower is cool enough to handle, wrap it tightly in the cloth so it can't spill out then, using your hands, squeeze very tightly to remove as much liquid as possible. It should feel dryish and be reduced in bulk. Return it to the food processor with the beans, eggs, salt and pepper and process until well combined but still with a little texture.

Divide the mixture into two equal portions and transfer each to a lined baking tray. Press each out to form a neat 25 cm (10 inch) round base. Scatter each with half the cherry tomatoes and olives and drizzle each with half the olive oil. Bake for 30 minutes or until the base is firm and golden. Scatter with cheese, then bake for another 10 minutes until the cheese is bubbling. Scatter with basil, season well and serve immediately.

You absolutely could use a couple of sheets of thawed frozen pastry here instead of making your own, but the flavor won't be anywhere near as good. Commercial pastries contain stabilizing ingredients and other additives, and most use baking margarine rather than butter. Oh, and they never have walnuts either, which give the base here lovely rich, nutty notes.

CAULIFLOWER, WALNUT AND SMOKED CHEESE TART

Serves 6

400 g (14 oz) large cauliflower florets
  (about 4 cm/1½ inches across)
225 g (8 oz/2⅓ cups) grated smoked cheddar cheese
2 large eggs, beaten well
1 egg yolk
250 ml (9 fl oz/1 cup) half-and-half (18% fat)
1 teaspoon salt
1 teaspoon freshly ground black pepper
10 sage leaves

WALNUT PASTRY
90 g (3¼ oz/¾ cup) walnuts, chopped
250 g (9 oz/1⅔ cups) whole-wheat flour
130 g (4½ oz/½ cup) cold unsalted butter, chopped
3 tablespoons iced water

For the walnut pastry, mix the walnuts in a food processor until finely ground. Add the flour and pulse to combine, then add the butter and pulse until the mixture resembles coarse breadcrumbs. Transfer to a large bowl, add the water and, using your hands, mix to form a firm dough. Add a little more water if necessary. Form the pastry into a disc, wrap in plastic wrap, then refrigerate for 30 minutes.

Steam the cauliflower over boiling water for 6 minutes or until nearly tender. Remove to a colander to cool.

On a lightly floured surface, roll the pastry out into a 45 x 17 cm (18 x 6½ inch) rectangle, 3 mm (⅛ inch) thick. Carefully transfer to a 34 x 11.5 cm (13½ x 4½ inch) non-stick tart pan with a removable base and ease it in. Don't worry too much if the pastry breaks (it is fragile)—you can patch up any broken areas, making sure you press them firmly together to join. Trim around the top of the tin. Refrigerate for 30 minutes to firm the pastry. Preheat the oven to 200°C (400°F).

Line the pastry with a piece of parchment paper, then fill with baking beads or dried beans. Bake for 10 minutes, then reduce the heat to 180°C (350°F) and bake for another 10 minutes. Remove the paper and beads and bake for a further 3–4 minutes or until dry to touch. Scatter with 125 g (4½ oz/1¼ cups) cheddar cheese, then scatter the cauliflower over the cheese.

Beat the eggs, yolk and half-and-half together in a bowl, add the salt and pepper, then carefully pour over the cauliflower. Scatter with the remaining cheese and the sage leaves and bake for 50 minutes or until set and golden. Cool slightly, then serve cut into slices.

There isn't much that ricotta can't do . . . except, maybe, broker world peace. It's as versatile as cauliflower and when you put these two ingredients together, you get fantastically tasty, and easy, recipes like this one. All this needs is a simple green salad on the side.

RICOTTA AND CAULIFLOWER PIE WITH TOMATO AND RED WINE SAUCE

Serves 4–6

80 ml (2½ fl oz/⅓ cup) extra virgin olive oil
60 g (2¼ oz/1 cup) fresh breadcrumbs
500 g (1 lb 2 oz/about ½ medium) cauliflower,
    trimmed and cut into large florets
690 g (1 lb 8 oz/3 cups) firm, fresh ricotta cheese
3 eggs, beaten well
35 g (1¼ oz/¼ cup) plain (all-purpose) flour
105 g (3¾ oz/¾ cup) grated mozzarella cheese
80 g (2¾ oz/¾ cup) grated parmesan cheese
1 teaspoon freshly grated nutmeg
2 teaspoons thyme leaves, chopped
1 teaspoon sea salt
1 teaspoon freshly ground black pepper

TOMATO AND RED WINE SAUCE
1½ tablespoons extra virgin olive oil
2 garlic cloves, finely chopped
1 onion, finely sliced
1 tablespoon tomato paste (concentrated purée)
125 ml (4 fl oz/½ cup) red wine
2 x 400 g (14-oz) cans chopped tomatoes
185 ml (6 fl oz/¾ cup) chicken stock
2 teaspoons sugar
3 teaspoons balsamic vinegar, or to taste

For the tomato and red wine sauce, heat the oil over medium heat in a saucepan. Add the garlic and onion and cook, stirring, for 7–8 minutes or until the onion has softened. Add the tomato paste and cook, stirring, for about 1 minute, then add the wine. Bring to a simmer and cook until the wine has reduced a little, then stir in the tomatoes and stock. Simmer over low heat for 10 minutes, stirring occasionally, then add the sugar and vinegar. Season to taste with sea salt and freshly ground black pepper and a little extra vinegar, if necessary.

Grease the base and sides of a 26 x 15 x 4 cm (10½ x 6 x 1½ inch) baking dish with 1 tablespoon of the olive oil, then scatter over about a third of the breadcrumbs. Steam the cauliflower over boiling water for 4–5 minutes or until nearly tender. Transfer to a colander and cool.

Preheat the oven to 180°C (350°F).

Combine the ricotta, eggs, flour, half the cheeses, nutmeg, thyme leaves, salt and pepper in a food processor and process until smooth. Pour into the baking dish, smoothing the surface even, then place the cauliflower over the top, pushing the florets in slightly but leaving the tops visible. Scatter over the remaining mozzarella and parmesan, then scatter over the remaining breadcrumbs. Drizzle over the remaining olive oil and bake for 1 hour or until puffed, golden and firm in the middle. Cool slightly, then cut into pieces and serve with the sauce spooned over.

These are really just a thinly veiled excuse to make scones, but you have to admit that cauliflower trim does make them look cute. Use any other cheese you like—a tasty cheddar would do just fine. So would feta, come to that.

CAULIFLOWER BLUE CHEESE SCONES

Makes 10 scones

20 small–medium cauliflower florets
370 g (13 oz/2½ cups) whole-wheat flour
5 teaspoons baking powder
1 teaspoon salt
50 g (1¾ oz/scant ¼ cup) unsalted butter, chopped
200 g (7 oz) gorgonzola cheese, chopped
2½ tablespoons finely chopped chives
300 ml (10½ fl oz) buttermilk, approximately

Preheat the oven to 220°C (425°F). Line a baking tray with parchment paper.

Steam the cauliflower over boiling water for 2–3 minutes or until the cauliflower is semi-cooked.

Stir together the flour, baking powder and salt in a bowl. Using your fingertips, rub in the butter until the mixture resembles fine breadcrumbs, then rub in half the gorgonzola. Stir in the chives, add the buttermilk and then, working quickly, stir with a flat-bladed knife to form a coarse, sticky dough. Add a little extra buttermilk if the mixture is too dry.

Turn out onto a floured board and, using your hands, lightly knead until the dough just comes together—take care not to overwork or the scones will be tough. Using your hands, pat out to a rough 20 x 15 cm (8 x 6 inch) rectangle, using a large knife to push the edges square. Cut out rounds with a 6.5 cm (2½ inch) cutter. Press together any scraps, re-roll and cut out more rounds—you should have 10. Press the remaining cheese gently into the scone tops. Press the cauliflower florets into the tops, stems down, then transfer to the baking tray.

Bake for 15 minutes or until risen, golden and cooked through. Transfer to a wire rack to cool. Scones are best served on the day they are made.

Add some finely chopped parsley or basil to the mix, or some very thinly sliced green onions (scallions) if you want to amp up the savory side of things. Tempting though it might be to rip into these while they're still hot, like many things, they taste best at room temperature. Slathered in butter, naturally.

CAULIFLOWER MUFFINS

Makes 12 muffins

400 g (14 oz/about ½ small) cauliflower,
    trimmed and cut into florets
250 ml (9 fl oz/1 cup) buttermilk
2 large eggs, beaten
4 tablespoons extra virgin olive oil
100 g (3½ oz/1 cup) grated parmesan cheese
2 teaspoons salt, or to taste
1 teaspoon freshly ground black pepper
335 g (12 oz/2¼ cups) plain (all-purpose) flour
5 teaspoons baking powder
100 g (3½ oz/1 cup) cheddar cheese
Chili flakes, for sprinkling

Preheat the oven to 180°C (350°F). Grease and flour a 12-hole muffin tin.

Finely chop 250 g (9 oz) of the cauliflower in a food processor. Finely slice the remaining cauliflower florets.

Add the buttermilk, eggs, oil, parmesan, salt and pepper to the processed cauliflower and stir well. Sift the flour and baking powder into another bowl, then add to the cauliflower mixture and quickly stir well—take care not to overmix or the muffins will be tough.

Divide into the muffin tins and top with the cheddar cheese. Scatter with the cauliflower slices and chili flakes, to taste. Bake for 25 minutes or until golden and cooked through. Cool in the pan for 5 minutes, then carefully turn out onto a wire rack to cool.

Shhhh—don't tell them there's cauli in these. They'll never, ever guess. It adds a little moisture, texture and natural sweetness and, of course, a dash of vegetable goodness.

CAULIFLOWER BROWNIES

Makes about 12 brownies

450 g (1 lb/about ½ small) cauliflower, trimmed and cut into small florets
200 g (7 oz) dark chocolate, chopped
125 g (4½ oz/½ cup) unsalted butter, chopped
3 large eggs
175 g (6 oz/½ cup) honey
200 g (7 oz/2 cups) ground almonds
55 g (2 oz/½ cup) cocoa powder
½ teaspoon baking powder

Steam the cauliflower over boiling water for 5–6 minutes or until tender. Cool in a colander.

Preheat the oven to 170°C (340°F). Grease and flour the sides of a 25.5 x 16.5 cm (10 x 6½ inch) baking pan and line with parchment paper.

Combine the chocolate and butter in a bowl over a saucepan of simmering water. Heat for 7–8 minutes or until melted, then stir until smooth. Remove from the heat and leave to cool.

Mix the cauliflower in a food processor until smooth.

Combine the eggs and honey and whisk with electric beaters on high speed for 6–7 minutes or until slightly thickened and creamy. Whisk in the chocolate mixture. Stir together the almonds, cocoa and baking powder in a bowl. Add to the chocolate mixture with the cooled cauliflower and stir well. Pour into the pan, smooth the surface and bake for 40 minutes or until firm. Cool in the pan for 10 minutes, then turn out onto a wire rack to cool.

Cut into pieces and store in the refrigerator in an airtight container—brownies will keep for up to 5 days.

Cauliflower brings its earthy sweetness to, yes, cheesecake. Really? You'll never even know it's there! Gild the lily by slathering the top with lashings of whipped cream, some toasted coconut and a sprinkling of finely grated lime zest just before you serve.

CAULIFLOWER, LIME AND COCONUT CHEESECAKE

Serves 8

200 g (7 oz) cauliflower florets
250 g (9 oz/generous 1 cup) cream cheese, chopped
300 g (10½ oz/1⅓ cups) firm, fresh ricotta cheese
150 g (5½ oz/⅔ cup) sugar
4 tablespoons lime juice
Finely grated zest of 2 limes
3 eggs, beaten well
45 g (1½ oz/½ cup) shredded coconut
2 tablespoons plain (all-purpose) flour
1 teaspoon coconut essence, or to taste

CHEESECAKE BASE
175 g (6 oz) plain sweet cookies, such as
   shortbread, broken
80 ml (2½ fl oz/⅓ cup) melted coconut oil
50 g (1¾ oz/½ cup) shredded coconut

For the cheesecake base, place the cookies in a food processor and mix to fine crumbs. With the motor running, add the oil and coconut and process until combined well. Press into the base of a 20 cm (8 inch) springform tin.

Preheat the oven to 170°C (340°F).

Steam the cauliflower over boiling water for 4 minutes or until tender, then cool in a colander. Process until very smooth, then add the cream cheese to the processor and mix until smooth, stopping to scrape the cream cheese down occasionally. Add the ricotta, sugar, lime juice and zest and process until smooth, then add the eggs, coconut, flour and essence and process until smooth.

Pour into the pan and bake for 50–60 minutes or until firm in the middle. Turn off the oven, open the door slightly, then leave until the cheesecake is completely cold.

BITS
PIC

AND
XLES

Along with spiralized zucchini, cauliflower "rice" is the faux carb of choice for many. Easy and delicious, it's so versatile. And there are a few ways you can cook it too, either by roasting, steaming or frying.

CAULIFLOWER "RICE"

Serves 4–6

700 g (1 lb 9 oz/about ½ medium) cauliflower, trimmed and chopped

Working in batches, process the cauliflower in a food processor until it resembles fine grains of rice. Now, you have a few options as to how to cook this:

Microwaving This is the easiest cooking method by far. Place the cauliflower in a heatproof bowl with just 1–2 tablespoons of water, cover tightly with plastic wrap, then microwave on high for about 3 minutes or until tender. If you don't own a microwave, cook the cauliflower with 80 ml (2½ fl oz/⅓ cup) water in a tightly covered saucepan over medium heat for about 5–6 minutes or until tender.

Roasting Spread the "rice" over a large baking tray, drizzle with olive oil and toss to coat lightly. Roast at 200°C (400°F) for 15 minutes, stirring it every now and then, or until tender and a little golden.

Stir-frying Heat 2 tablespoons of peanut, vegetable or coconut oil in a large wok over medium–high heat, add the cauliflower and stir-fry for 5 minutes or until tender. You can cook the cauliflower with chopped chili, garlic or ginger, add some finely sliced green onions (scallions) and/or chopped herbs, such as cilantro, mint, parsley or basil.

The sauces and garnishes here are a gala way to serve the whole roast cauli, but actually you could dish it up plain. Or smothered in any favorite sauce—cheese, hollandaise, pesto or chimichurri, for example. Zhoug is a classic Yemeni green chili sauce; you can adjust the heat to suit your tolerance for spice. Serve the cauli cut into wedges with roasts, grills, poached chicken or salmon or whatever you darned well fancy.

WHOLE ROAST CAULIFLOWER WITH ZHOUG, TAHINI CREAM AND POMEGRANATE

Serves 4–6

1.5 liters (52 fl oz/6 cups) chicken or vegetable stock
1.2 kg (2 lb 10 oz/about 1 large) cauliflower, trimmed
    but leaves left attached if you prefer
2½ tablespoons slivered almonds, toasted
Seeds of 1 pomegranate

TAHINI CREAM
3 garlic cloves, finely chopped
1 teaspoon ground cumin
2½ tablespoons lemon juice
205 g (7¼ oz/¾ cup) tahini
125 ml (4 fl oz/½ cup) water

ZHOUG
1½ teaspoons caraway seeds
8 medium green chilies, chopped
6 garlic cloves, chopped
1 teaspoon ground cumin
½ teaspoon ground cardamom
2 large handfuls of cilantro
Large handful of flat-leaf parsley leaves
2½ tablespoons lemon juice
125 ml (4 fl oz/½ cup) extra virgin olive oil
1 teaspoon sea salt
1 teaspoon freshly ground black pepper

For the tahini cream, combine all the ingredients in a food processor until smooth and creamy, adding extra water if it is too thick. Season to taste with sea salt and freshly ground black pepper.

For the zhoug, using a spice grinder or a mortar and pestle, coarsely grind the caraway seeds. Transfer to a food processor with the remaining ingredients and process until a coarse paste forms. Season to taste.

Preheat the oven to 180°C (350°F).

Bring the stock to the boil in a saucepan large enough to hold the cauliflower. Add the cauliflower with the leaves still attached, cover, then cook over medium–high heat for 15–20 minutes or until partially cooked through. Drain well, reserving the cooking liquid.

Transfer the cauliflower to a large, deep roasting dish with 500 ml (17 fl oz/2 cups) of the reserved liquid. Roast for 40–50 minutes, adding a little extra stock if the liquid evaporates, or until the cauliflower is tender and golden. Transfer to a serving dish. Spoon the tahini cream over, then spoon over the zhoug. Scatter over the almonds and pomegranate seeds then serve, cut into wedges.

Cauliflower cheese is maybe the classic way to cook cauliflower. The idea is believed to have originated in Cyprus (once an English colony), where cooking with béchamel sauce was common. Cyprus is also thought to be the place where cauliflower itself originated. In any case, it's hard to improve on an iconic dish but, if you want to mix things up a bit, use half broccoli/half cauliflower. Or add some powdered mustard, chopped chives, anchovies or Tabasco to the sauce.

CAULIFLOWER CHEESE

Serves 4–6

40 g (1½ oz/scant ¼ cup) butter
40 g (1½ oz/¼ cup) plain (all-purpose) flour
600 ml (21 fl oz/2⅓ cups) milk, heated
Large pinch of grated nutmeg
100 ml (3½ fl oz) half-and-half (18% fat)
200 g (7 oz) aged Gruyère, grated
2 egg yolks
800 g (1 lb 12 oz/1 small) cauliflower, trimmed
and cut into large florets

Preheat the oven to 180°C (350°F).

Melt the butter over medium heat in a large saucepan then, using a whisk, add the flour, stirring until smooth. Whisking constantly to avoid lumps forming, add the milk about 125 ml (4 fl oz/½ cup) at a time, bringing the mixture to a simmer before adding any more milk. Cook, whisking often, for 5–6 minutes, then season to taste with sea salt, freshly ground black pepper and the nutmeg. Remove from the heat and stir in the half-and-half, 100 g (3½ oz) of the cheese and the egg yolks.

Meanwhile, steam the cauliflower over boiling water for 7–8 minutes or until cooked but still a little firm. Transfer to a baking dish, pour over the sauce and scatter over the remaining cheese. Bake for 20 minutes or until bubbling and the cheese is golden.

This is great with a steak or a piece of grilled lamb (medium-rare, please!) or with anything that you'd routinely serve with mashed potato. As a variation, and if you prefer the flavor, use half butter and half oil and throw in some chopped herbs (parsley or chives, for example) or perhaps a little freshly grated nutmeg, right at the end. For an even creamier mash, purée the mixture with a can of drained, rinsed butter beans.

ROAST CAULIFLOWER AND GARLIC MASH

Serves 4

60 ml (2 fl oz/¼ cup) extra virgin olive oil
1 large head of garlic
800 g (1 lb 12 oz/about 1 small) cauliflower, trimmed
50 g (1¾ oz/¼ cup) butter

Preheat the oven to 200°C (400°F). Drizzle half the olive oil over the base of a large baking dish.

Cut the garlic in half widthways and place, cut side down, in the dish. Chop the cauliflower into small florets and place in the tray. Cover the tray tightly with foil, then bake for 50–60 minutes or until the cauliflower and garlic are both very tender.

Squeeze the garlic from the skins, then transfer to a food processor with the cauliflower and the butter and process until smooth. Season well with sea salt and freshly ground black pepper.

Another versatile, easy side that you'll love having in your repertoire. Fennel takes on far mellower notes when it's cooked, so if you're not fond of its aniseed strength when raw, rest assured it's sweet and smooth tasting here.

CAULIFLOWER AND FENNEL PUREE

Serves 6

80 g (2¾ oz/⅓ cup) butter
400 g (14 oz/about 1 large) fennel bulb,
    trimmed and chopped
600 g (1 lb 5 oz/about ½ medium) cauliflower,
    trimmed and chopped
400 g (14 oz/about 2) red-skinned or other all-purpose
    potatoes, peeled and chopped
1 tablespoon lemon juice, or to taste
Small handful of dill, chopped

Melt the butter in a large saucepan over medium–low heat, add the fennel and cauliflower then stir to combine. Cover the pan then cook, stirring occasionally and adding a few tablespoons of water if the vegetables stick, for about 35 minutes or until the vegetables are tender.

Meanwhile, cook the potato in boiling, salted water for 12–15 minutes or until tender. Drain well. Push the potato through a potato ricer, or mash using a potato masher, until smooth. Transfer the fennel and cauliflower mixture to a food processor then process until smooth. Return to the pan with the potato, lemon juice and chopped dill and stir over low heat for 2–3 minutes or until heated through. Season with sea salt and freshly ground black pepper.

While you don't absolutely need to soak the split peas, this does speed up the cooking time. The great thing about this dhal? You can easily double the recipe for a crowd or freeze the extra to have on hand when you're pushed for cooking time. Serve the dhal as a side with your fave Indian dish, alongside a piece of grilled fish or steak or as a vegetarian main, with purchased chutneys, naan bread, poppadoms and steamed basmati rice on the side. Yum.

CAULIFLOWER DHAL

Serves 4

280 g (10 oz/1¼ cups) yellow split peas
2 tablespoons vegetable oil
1 teaspoon yellow mustard seeds
900 g (2 lb/about 1 small–medium) cauliflower, trimmed and cut into 1 cm (½ inch) pieces
2 garlic cloves, finely chopped
1½ tablespoons finely chopped fresh ginger
¼ teaspoon ground turmeric
1 teaspoon cumin seeds
2 medium green chilies, thinly sliced
20 curry leaves
250 ml (9 fl oz/1 cup) coconut milk
1 teaspoon sea salt, or to taste
2 tablespoons lime juice, or to taste

Place the split peas in a large bowl, cover with cold water, then soak for 2 hours. Drain well then combine in a large saucepan with 875 ml (30 fl oz/3½ cups) water. Bring to a boil, skimming off any scum that rises to the surface. Simmer over medium heat for 25 minutes or until the peas are tender and the mixture is thick but still a little soupy. Remove from the heat.

While the split peas are cooking, heat the oil in a large saucepan over medium heat. Add the mustard seeds and cook for 1–2 minutes or until they pop. Add the cauliflower, stir well, then cover and cook for 13 minutes, stirring often, or until the cauliflower is tender.

Add the garlic, ginger, turmeric and cumin seeds and cook, stirring often, for 3 minutes or until fragrant. Add the green chilies, curry leaves, coconut milk, salt and split peas and stir well. Bring to a simmer over low heat then cook, stirring often so the dhal doesn't stick and burn, for 15 minutes or until thickened slightly. Stir in the lime juice and season to taste with sea salt and freshly ground black pepper.

Rich, with zingy, relish-like flavors, this Sicilian vegetable dish is endlessly versatile. You can serve it on bruschetta, as a sauce for pasta, with mozzarella for a pizza topping or as an accompaniment to grilled or roasted meats. While all the sautéing of each veggie separately might seem a chore, it does give the best flavor. If you want to speed things up, just get a few pans going at the same time.

CAULIFLOWER CAPONATA

Serves 6

1 eggplant (about 450 g/1 lb), trimmed and cut into 2.5 cm (1 inch) pieces
1 tablespoon sea salt
Olive oil, for cooking
3 celery stalks, cut into 2.5 cm (1 inch) pieces
2 zucchini, cut into 2.5 cm (1 inch) pieces
1 large green pepper, trimmed, seeded and cut into 2.5 cm (1 inch) pieces
400 g (14 oz/about ½ small) cauliflower, trimmed and cut into florets
2 onions, cut into 2.5 cm (1 inch) pieces
3 garlic cloves, chopped
60 g (2¼ oz/⅓ cup) raisins
6 anchovy fillets
1 tablespoon tomato paste (concentrated purée)
2 x 400 g (14-oz) cans chopped tomatoes
80 ml (2½ fl oz/⅓ cup) chicken stock or water
2 tablespoons red wine or balsamic vinegar
3 teaspoons sugar, or to taste
85 g (3 oz/½ cup) stuffed green olives, coarsely chopped
50 g (1¾ oz/¼ cup) drained baby capers
Handful of mint leaves, coarsely chopped
Handful of basil leaves, coarsely chopped

Layer the eggplant in a colander, scattering with about 3 teaspoons of the salt as you go. Leave for 30 minutes to give up some of its juices, then rinse. Drain, then transfer to a clean dish towel to absorb as much water as possible.

Meanwhile, heat 1½ tablespoons oil in a large, non-stick pan over medium heat. Add the celery then cook, stirring occasionally, for 7–8 minutes or until softened and starting to turn golden. Remove to a bowl, keeping as much of the oil in the pan as you can.

Return the pan to medium heat, then add the zucchini with a little extra oil, if necessary. Cook the zucchini, tossing occasionally, for 4 minutes or until softened and light golden—add to the celery in the bowl. Cook the pepper over medium heat for 6–7 minutes, adding a little more oil if necessary, until softened and golden, then add to the vegetables in the bowl. Repeat with the cauliflower florets, cooking for 8 minutes or until starting to soften and light golden. Cook the eggplant for 8 minutes or until golden and softened, then add to the vegetables.

While the vegetables are cooking, heat 2½ tablespoons of oil in a large saucepan over medium heat, add the onion and garlic and cook, stirring often, for 6–7 minutes or until softened and light golden. Add the raisins, anchovies and tomato paste and cook, stirring, for 1 minute, then add the tomatoes, stock, the vegetables in the bowl, vinegar, sugar, olives and capers. Season to taste, then bring to a simmer. Cover and cook over low heat for 10–15 minutes or until the vegetables are tender. Stir in the mint and basil leaves before serving.

Actually, if you fry some slices of haloumi (cut them about 1.5 cm/⅝ inch thick, dust lightly in flour and cook in olive oil over medium heat for about 3 minutes on each side), you can turn this dish into a good simple meal. Otherwise, serve it as a side with your favorite meats or as part of a larger North African-inspired spread.

MOROCCAN CAULIFLOWER WITH TOMATO AND OLIVES

Serves 4

100 ml (3½ fl oz) extra virgin olive oil
800 g (1 lb 12 oz/about 1 small) cauliflower, trimmed and cut into florets
4 garlic cloves, thinly sliced
½ cinnamon stick
1½ teaspoons sweet paprika
1 teaspoon ground ginger
½ teaspoon ground turmeric
½ teaspoon ground chili, or to taste
600 g (1 lb 5 oz/about 3 large) tomatoes, cut into wedges
125 ml (4 fl oz/½ cup) chicken stock or water
1 tablespoon honey
2½ tablespoons lemon juice
2 tablespoons chopped flat-leaf parsley
40 g (1½ oz/⅓ cup) pitted green olives
½ preserved lemon, pulp discarded, rinsed and chopped

Heat 3 tablespoons of the oil in a large, deep, frying pan or flameproof casserole over medium heat. Add the cauliflower then cook, stirring often, for 15–20 minutes or until the cauliflower is golden and almost cooked.

Heat the remaining oil in another pan over medium heat, add the garlic and cook, stirring, for 3 minutes or until softened. Add the spices and cook, stirring, for 1–2 minutes or until fragrant, then add the tomato, stock and honey and bring to a simmer. Add to the cauliflower in the pan with the lemon juice and bring to a simmer. Cover and cook for 7–8 minutes or until the cauliflower is tender and the tomatoes are soft.

Stir in the parsley, parsley, olives and preserved lemon and season with sea salt and freshly ground black pepper.

Here's a spin on the classic layered eggplant dish that's associated with southern Italy and is particularly popular in Naples. Crumbed, fried cauliflower is perfect as the main ingredient, with the panko (don't use any other type of dried breadcrumb) forming a lovely crunchy crust.

CAULIFLOWER PARMIGIANA

Serves 6

1.2 kg (2 lb 10 oz/about 1 large) cauliflower, trimmed
2 large eggs, beaten well
60 ml (2 fl oz/¼ cup) buttermilk
120 g (4¼ oz/2 cups) panko breadcrumbs
Olive oil spray
Large handful of basil leaves, torn
250 g (9 oz/2 cups) grated mozzarella cheese
70 g (2½ oz/⅔ cup) grated parmesan cheese

TOMATO SAUCE
2½ tablespoons olive oil
1 large onion, finely chopped
2 garlic cloves, finely chopped
1 tablespoon tomato paste (concentrated purée)
2 x 400 g (14-oz) cans chopped tomatoes
170 ml (5½ fl oz/⅔ cup) chicken stock
250 ml (9 fl oz/1 cup) tomato passata (puréed tomatoes)
1 tablespoon balsamic vinegar, or to taste
2–3 teaspoons sugar, or to taste

For the tomato sauce, heat the oil in a large saucepan over medium heat, add the onion and garlic and cook, stirring, for 5–6 minutes, or until the onion has softened. Add the tomato paste and cook, stirring, for 1 minute, then add the chopped tomatoes, chicken stock, passata, balsamic and 2 teaspoons of the sugar and season to taste with sea salt and freshly ground black pepper. Bring to a simmer then cook over low heat, stirring occasionally, for 20 minutes or until reduced and thickened slightly. Add a little more vinegar or sugar, if necessary.

Meanwhile, preheat the oven to 180°C (350°F) and line two baking trays with parchment paper. Using a large, sharp knife, cut the cauliflower lengthways through the core into slices about 1.5 cm (⅝ inch) thick, creating as many large slices as possible.

Whisk the eggs and buttermilk in a large bowl until smooth. Place the panko in a large dish. Working with one piece of cauliflower at a time, dip in the egg mixture, turning it to coat and allowing excess to drain off. Dip in the panko, pressing the crumbs onto the cauliflower to coat all over.

Arrange the coated cauliflower on the tray, then spray generously with olive oil. Bake for 20 minutes or until light golden. Turn over, spray with oil and cook for 15 minutes or until cooked through.

Spread the hot tomato sauce in a large baking dish then scatter with the basil. Place the cauliflower over the sauce, overlapping it slightly if necessary to cover. Season well with salt and pepper then scatter with the cheese. Bake for 20 minutes or until the cauliflower is heated through and the cheese is bubbling and golden. Serve immediately.

Mustard seeds and mustard oil are liberally used in Bengali cookery, but the oil can be pungent and must be heated well to eliminate some of its strong odor. It has a cultural as well as culinary significance in India, where it is important at events such as weddings.

CAULIFLOWER WITH TAMARIND AND MUSTARD SEEDS

Serves 4

1 tablespoon yellow mustard seeds
1 teaspoon ground turmeric
2 tablespoons tamarind purée
3 tablespoons mustard oil
600 g (1 lb 5 oz/about ½ medium) cauliflower, trimmed and cut into small florets
2 garlic cloves, finely chopped
1 small onion, finely chopped
3 small green chilies, chopped
2–3 teaspoons nigella seeds

Using a spice grinder or mortar and pestle, grind or pound the mustard seeds to a powder. Stir well in a bowl with the turmeric, tamarind and 125 ml (4 fl oz/½ cup) water.

Heat the oil in a large, heavy-based pan over medium heat, then add the cauliflower, in batches if necessary, and cook, stirring, for 6 minutes or until it starts to turn golden. Remove to a bowl, reserving the pan.

Add the garlic, onion and chili to the pan, adding a little extra oil if necessary, and cook, stirring, for 5–6 minutes or until the onion is light golden.

Return the cauliflower mixture to the pan, add the tamarind mixture and nigella seeds and bring to a simmer. Cover and cook for 5 minutes or until the cauliflower is cooked through, adding a little water if starting to stick—it should be quite dry when the cauliflower is cooked. If there is liquid remaining, remove the lid and simmer until nearly all evaporated. Season well with sea salt and freshly ground black pepper.

We all need a few simple vegetable side dish recipes in our repertoire; ones we can whip up with ease at a moment's notice. With some cauliflower and a few staples at your easy disposal, this dish fits that bill. It's excellent served with quickly cooked meats such as a steak, lamb chops or salmon.

CHILI CAULIFLOWER

Serves 4

600 g (1 lb 5 oz/about ½ medium) cauliflower,
    trimmed and cut into small florets
60 g (2¼ oz/¼ cup) butter, chopped
1½ tablespoons tomato paste (concentrated purée)
½ teaspoon chili flakes, or to taste
Small handful of cilantro leaves, chopped
½ teaspoon sea salt, or to taste
1 teaspoon freshly ground black pepper

Steam the cauliflower over boiling water for 8 minutes or until tender. When it has nearly finished cooking, heat the butter in a large frying pan over medium heat until it starts to sizzle. Stir in the tomato paste and chili and cook, stirring to combine well, for 1 minute. Add the cauliflower, cilantro, salt and pepper and toss to coat.

Serve with cheddar, cured meats and bread for a plowman's type of arrangement, or alongside simply cooked fish or meats. If you don't want to mess around with jar sterilization, no judgement. Just cool the pickle and store the mixture in a scrupulously clean plastic container in the fridge, where it will happily keep for 2 or so months.

DILL AND ALLSPICE PICKLED CAULIFLOWER

Makes about 1.25 liters (44 fl oz/ 5 cups)

500 ml (17 fl oz/2 cups) red wine vinegar
185 g (6½ oz/generous ¾ cup) sugar
3 teaspoons dill seeds
3 teaspoons whole allspice berries, crushed
2 fresh bay leaves, bruised
400 g (14 oz) cauliflower florets
Handful of dill fronds

Put the vinegar, sugar, dill seeds, allspice and bay leaves in a saucepan. Stir over medium heat for 5 minutes or until the sugar has dissolved. Bring to a simmer and add the cauliflower. Cook over medium–low heat for 5–6 minutes or until nearly tender—the cauliflower should be a little firm.

Spoon the cauliflower into hot, sterilized jars and pour the liquid over the top. Seal while still hot. The cauliflower will keep for up to 3 months if stored in a cool, dark place.

In Malaysia they serve this as a side dish with grills, rice dishes and even satay. This is loosely based on the flavors you'd find in Penang, Malaysia, home to some of Asia's best food. If you don't want this much achar on your hands, just halve the recipe.

MALAY CAULIFLOWER PICKLE (ACHAR)

Makes about 1.5 liters (52 fl oz/ 6 cups)

40 g (1½ oz/¼ cup) sesame seeds
2 Lebanese (short) cucumbers, halved
    lengthways and seeded
1½ teaspoons salt
2 small carrots, cut into thin rounds
500 g (1 lb 2 oz/about ½ medium) cauliflower,
    trimmed and cut into small florets
2 long, thin Japanese eggplants,
    trimmed and cut into 1 cm (½ inch) thick rounds
2 tablespoons vegetable oil
5 garlic cloves, thinly sliced
6 red Asian shallots, sliced
100 ml (3½ fl oz/scant ½ cup) white wine vinegar
55 g (2 oz/¼ cup) sugar
50 g (1¾ oz/⅓ cup) unsalted roasted peanuts
Cilantro sprigs, to serve

PICKLE PASTE
1 tablespoon belacan (Malaysian shrimp paste)
15 dried red chilies, soaked in boiling water for
    30 minutes, then drained
8 candlenuts, chopped
2 tablespoons chopped fresh turmeric
2 tablespoons chopped galangal

Toast the sesame seeds in a small, heavy-based dry frying pan for a few minutes, then set aside.

For the pickle paste, wrap the belacan in foil then toast in the frying pan over medium heat for 2 minutes on each side or until fragrant. Cool, then mix in a food processor with the remaining ingredients until smooth.

Cut the cucumbers into 2.5 cm (1 inch) thick slices, then combine in a colander with the salt, tossing to coat. Leave for 20 minutes to drain and soften. Transfer to a clean dish towel to dry.

Bring a saucepan of salted water to the boil. Add the carrot and cook for 2 minutes or beginning to soften but still has some bite. Remove to a colander with a slotted spoon and drain well. Add the cauliflower to the boiling water and cook for 2 minutes or until just softened, then transfer to a colander with a slotted spoon and drain well. Repeat with the eggplant. Keep 80 ml (2½ fl oz/⅓ cup) of cooking water.

Heat the oil in a wok over medium heat, add the paste, garlic and shallots and stir-fry for 3 minutes or until fragrant. Add the vinegar, sugar and reserved water and bring to a simmer. Add the vegetables and stir well. Cook, stirring gently to prevent breaking up, for 4 minutes or until the vegetables are just tender. Add the peanuts and remove from the heat. Cool to room temperature, then serve scattered with sesame seeds and cilantro sprigs. Will keep, refrigerated, for up to 1 week.

Piccalilli was England's culinary response to Indian pickles and it's thought to date from the mid-eighteenth century. Its traditional use is as an accompaniment to foods such as grilled meats, sausages, raised pies, ham and feisty cheeses.

PICCALILLI

Makes about 1 liter (35 fl oz/ 4 cups)

300 g (10½ oz) small cauliflower florets
1 small Lebanese (short) cucumber,
    cut into 5 mm (¼ inch) pieces
100 g (3½ oz) green beans, trimmed and cut
    into 2 cm (¾ inch) pieces
1 onion, chopped
1 carrot, chopped
1 celery stalk, trimmed and chopped
2 tablespoons salt
125 g (4½ oz/generous ½ cup) sugar
3 teaspoons powdered mustard
1 teaspoon ground turmeric
1 red chili, chopped
500 ml (17 fl oz/2 cups) white wine vinegar
35 g (1¼ oz/¼ cup) plain (all-purpose) flour

Combine the cauliflower, cucumber, beans, onion, carrot, celery and salt in a large bowl. Add enough water to cover the vegetables, cover with a plate to keep them submerged, then stand overnight. Drain the vegetables well, then rinse under cold running water. Drain well again.

Combine the vegetables with the sugar, mustard, turmeric, chili and 300 ml (10½ fl oz) of the vinegar in a large saucepan. Bring to a simmer, removing any scum that rises to the surface, then simmer for 3 minutes. In a small bowl, whisk together the flour with the remaining vinegar until a smooth paste forms. Stir into the mixture on the stove then, stirring constantly to avoid lumps forming, bring it to a simmer. Cook for 1–2 minutes or until the mixture thickens, then remove from the heat.

While still hot, spoon into hot sterilized jars and seal. Store in a cool dark place for 1 month to allow flavors to develop before using. Piccalilli will keep, stored in a cool dark place, for up to 12 months.

INDEX

AcKNOWLEDGMєNTS

To Diana Hill, Vivien Valk, Jane Price, Henrietta Ashton, Alissa Dinallo
and Kay Halsey of Murdoch Books—if there is a Dream Team of
creatives, editors, organizers and visionaries, you guys are surely it.

Thank you for letting me loose on this glorious project and for making
it look so stunning and read so well.

And thanks too to my wonderful family, Andrew and Harry, who now
love cauliflower as much as I do.

Copyright © Murdoch Books, 2019.

First Published by Murdoch Books Australia, an
imprint of Allen & Unwin, in 2018 as *Cauliflower Is
King*.

First Skyhorse Publishing edition 2019.

Skyhorse Publishing books may be purchased in
bulk at special discounts for sales promotion,
corporate gifts, fund-raising, or educational
purposes. Special editions can also be created
to specifications. For details, contact the Special
Sales Department, Skyhorse Publishing, 307 West
36th Street, 11th Floor, New York, NY 10018 or
info@skyhorsepublishing.com.

Skyhorse® and Skyhorse Publishing® are registered
trademarks of Skyhorse Publishing, Inc.®, a Delaware
corporation. Visit our website at
www.skyhorsepublishing.com.

10 9 8 7 6 5 4 3 2

Library of Congress Cataloging-in-Publication Data is
available on file.

Editorial management by Jane Price
Design management by Vivien Valk
Design by Alissa Dinallo
Interior illustrations by Alissa Dinallo and Kitty Clement
Interior Photography by Leanne Kitchen
Cover photography credit: Shutterstock
Style merchandizing by Sarah O'Brien
Production directing by Lou Playfair

ISBN: 978-1-5107-4554-4
eBook ISBN: 978-1-5107-4568-1

Printed in China